PRAISE FOR SPIRITU

"In *Spiritual Fitness,* Dr. Mramor presents a very workable program for achieving Spiritual Fitness. I especially appreciate her emphasis on daily practice, so different from our usual ideal of instant enlightenment. I recommend this book to those who aspire to deepen their sense of spiritual connectedness, whether because of illness or challenge in life or just because it's important."

— Sr. Helen Prejean, C.S.J.
author, *Dead Man Walking*

"In this integration of mainstream psychology and spirituality, Nancy Mramor provides her readers with a practical program with a practical program that may well enrich their lives. *Spiritual Fitness* is written for readers of all faiths, as well as for those with no formal religious affiliation at all. Its exercises, affirmations, and prayers provide a regimen designed to help nourish the soul as well as inspire day-by-day behavior."

— Stanley Krippner, Ph.D.
co-author, *Extraordinary Dreams and How to Use Them*
Professor of Psychology, Saybrook Graduate School
and Research Center

"In *Spiritual Fitness,* Dr. Mramor emphasizes the importance of daily practice, of getting spiritually fit in the same way one would approach physical fitness . . . the idea of perseverance, prioritizing, and making commitments apply equally."

— Lewis Mehl-Madrona, M.D., Ph.D.
author, *Coyote Medicine*

"*Spiritual Fitness* is a highly effective and profound method of spiritual transformation in which I have great interest. Nancy's path to Spiritual Fitness will heal your mind, body, and emotions, while confirming the presence of the spiritual world. This loving work is inspirational and powerful."

— Suzanne Caplan
author, speaker, consultant

ABOUT THE AUTHOR

Nancy Mramor (Pennsylvania) is a licensed psychologist specializing in holistic psychology. Her unique spiritual fitness program is based upon twenty-nine years of professional experience. Dr. Mramor's *Mastering Relaxation* curriculum was proven effective and has been well received internationally. She has taught Spiritual Fitness techniques at conferences, universities, and hospitals throughout the U.S. and in Europe.

EMBRACE YOUR SOUL, TRANSFORM YOUR LIFE

Spiritual

Fitness

NANCY MRAMOR, PH.D.

Llewellyn Publications
St. Paul, Minnesota

First Edition
First Printing, 2004

Author photo by Harry Giglio
Cover images ©2004 by Digital Vision & PhotoDisc
Cover design by Kevin R. Brown

The people and experiences in this book are true, yet some of the details have been changed to protect their privacy and confidentiality.

Library of Congress Cataloging-in-Publication Data
Mramor, Nancy, 1954 –
    Spiritual fitness : embrace your soul, transform your life / Nancy Mramor. — 1st ed.
      p. cm.
    Includes index.
    ISBN 0-7387-0640-X
    1. Spiritual life. 2. Spirituality. I. Title: Embrace your soul, transform your life. II. Title.

BL624.M73 2005
204'.4—dc22   2004059610

Llewellyn Publications
A Division of Llewellyn Worldwide, Ltd.
P.O. Box 64383, Dept. 0-7387-0640-X
St. Paul, MN 55164-0383, U.S.A.
www.llewellyn.com

Llewellyn is a registered trademark of Llewellyn Worldwide, Ltd.

Printed in the United States of America

ALSO BY NANCY MRAMOR, PH.D.

Mastering Relaxation

CONTENTS

EXERCISES

ACKNOWLEDGMENTS

I wish to thank:

Linda Hilliard for starting me on the path of Spiritual Fitness.

Jesus, Buddha, Abraham, Moses, Muhammed, and all of the spiritual leaders for paving their paths to God.

Lee Gutkind for showing up in my life with his guidance and wisdom.

Irene Prokop for her expertise at critical times in the writing process.

Linda Cardimen for always, always believing in me.

Dr. Capers for his healing when it was needed most.

My angels for their daily guidance in my life.

INTRODUCTION
TO SPIRITUAL FITNESS

How and Why to Use This Book

They say that it is not the soul that struggles first
touched by God, but this Universe of Love which
is fishing for us.

—Sophy Burnam

OUR LONGING FOR CONTACT with some mystical deity
and the deity's longing for us to meet it is a force that
leads us into essential transformation. It is like the
caterpillar longing to be what it is already, an unman-
ifested butterfly. This longing is what drives us toward
experiences that transform us spiritually. The power
of these experiences so moves us that our spirits soar
to the top of our priority lists and we are never the
same. Thank God! That is what happens on our journey to Spiritual Fitness.

The journey uses practices that will heal your heart,
quiet and expand your mind, and increase physical

health and fitness by attending primarily and fore-
mostly to your spirit. The information in this book may
hold the most critical keys to your personal and spiritual growth. Your growth and happiness may depend
upon it!

As a psychotherapist who has used Spiritual Fitness
techniques extensively for twenty-nine years, both personally and with adults and children, I know the benefits of approaching life from a spiritual perspective. As a
doctor of psychology, I have incorporated hypnosis,
yoga, meditation, prayer, visualization, intuitive development, dream interpretation, medical intuition, holistic psychotherapy, and other techniques into a program
of Spiritual Fitness for myself and for others in classes
and psychotherapy. I have learned to listen to my inner
voice, seen my life purpose, moved toward it, experienced results, and helped others to do the same. Having taught Spiritual Fitness to people from preschool
to graduate school and into the golden years, I know
how well they work. I have incorporated them into the
media, as well, in television, radio, and print, and I
currently work with local television stations to produce segments on health, education, and Spiritual Fitness.

Educators, holistically oriented therapists, parents,
single people, married people, physicians, nurses, and
individuals interested in a spiritual approach to life
have benefited from Spiritual Fitness. Those with a
strong adherence to a specific religion have enriched
their faith. Those with a universal belief in God have
embraced Spiritual Fitness as a way of life.

Spiritual Fitness addresses many of the issues of purpose in life: self-fulfillment, psychological issues, health issues and relationship issues. Examining your relationship to money, to people, to yourself, and to your spirit provides an avenue to have greater success in all areas. You may even redefine success in your life in a whole new way.

The Spiritual Fitness curriculum for children was especially well received internationally and research showed that it reduced observable symptoms of stress in children. The American Psychological Association invited me to share the adult program at their women's health conference. Countless hospitals, school districts, parent groups, private individuals, and athletes have incorporated these techniques for personal growth and personal success. For all of these reasons, I was on fire to put all of this information into a book.

As you read this book, you will be likely to hear that which is salient or relevant for you at this point in your awareness, but not hear that which does not connect to your experiences. If parts of this book are brought to your attention later, you may not even remember reading them, for that is how our minds work. The exercises in this book are about removing the static from your view of life and letting go of pessimism, disbelief, negativity, or blocks in yourself that interfere with personal happiness. They stand in the way of the knowledge of your own inner spirit.

The journey to Spiritual Fitness will take as long as it takes for you, for most of us a lifetime. After all, that is the purpose of being in this life: to rediscover and come back home to ourselves, our higher selves, our best selves. Many skills are needed to reach our goal and there are many fine tools available for the journey. The ones I will share in this book are those I have found to be most effective and those that keep us closest to our spiritual selves.

My journey to Spiritual Fitness began in an Italian Catholic family. I felt a strong sense of joy during the beginning years of my life, abundantly happy to be in the world, and in my body. I felt the fullness of my spirit, and moved exuberantly, overflowing with a sense of something much greater than myself. I later came to identify the source of this energy as my spirit within myself. I lost touch with my joyful spirit as I got older, creating an emptiness in myself, but began a spiritual journey to rediscover my spirit. The road back has helped me to heal many parts of myself, through the tools I will share in Spiritual Fitness. The tools have proved enlightening and empowering for me and many others and are used by many holistically oriented therapists.

Many paths will take us where we want to go. At times, we experience a feeling of our higher self through our religion. In this book I describe various religious experiences in formal settings, because the presence of God is strong there and spiritual manifestations often occur. We can also get in touch with our paths through dreams, color, music, sound, dietary practice, exercises, self-hypnosis, and visualization. Meditation and prayer profoundly swirl our feet dancing onto the path, and intuition and self-awareness are ongoing processes of development. In modern spiritualism, these intuitive awarenesses are one of the purposes for meditation, where in Buddhism, they are merely a distraction to becoming internally quiet. Whichever path is part of your plan is the right one for you. Later, I will describe the use of sensory awareness and self-hypnosis as ways to discover what is the best process for you. I will examine each of these tools for experiencing Spiritual Fitness and see how each might serve your purpose.

Becoming spiritually fit is not accomplished by using a single technique or method. Spiritual Fitness is about following a path of experience that provides a wealth of choices. I present various techniques that have universal effectiveness. When used in combination, these techniques can bring one to health and fitness of mind, body, and emotions. This is accomplished in a manner far more fulfilling than could ever be accomplished through any individual practice done in isolation.

Getting spiritually fit may mean giving up old ways of doing things which have not produced the results that you wanted, or produced them with only partial success. On the other hand, you will bring with you any growth, past experience, education, or awareness that is working for you and will continue to assist you. As you are reading, you may even now be beginning to mentally review your life to see what has or has not worked for you.

As I share with you the pathway to Spiritual Fitness, I will offer personal stories of mine and others' experiences about intuitive awarenesses, communications from deceased loved ones, out-of-body experiences, and intuitive messages which were by-products of my own spiritual path.

These stories are woven into a tapestry of a plan for becoming spiritually fit and happy that anyone can follow. Achieving Spiritual Fitness is much like achieving any other type of fitness. You don't just go out and run a marathon after six months of inactivity. The same is true with Spiritual Fitness. You work with breathing and movement to quiet the mind and open up energy of your body. You acquire the awareness and experiences which form the threads that weave your own tapestry of an enlightened self. This tapestry provides a fullness and a warmth from which to live.

The book comes at a time in my life when I have used the techniques to save my own life. In the final chapter of the book, you will understand how I integrated the techniques to face a life challenge that proved to be the greatest test on the path of Spiritual Fitness that I ever encountered.

Begin the path to Spiritual Fitness by working with the tools and exercises in each chapter. In order to do that, set aside time to do the following:

1. Keep a daily journal. Pick a time each day when you will write in it and read it and be as consistent as possible. Any time of day when you can be consistent is the best time for you, whether that is morning, evening, after work, or lunch.

First, put down anything that you are thinking, reflections from the past twenty-four hours, ideas, or desires. In this way you clear your mind to do the exercises in each chapter. Record all of the exercises from the book in the journal. This will include recording your affirmations and prayers when you get to the chapters that include exercises for developing them. These prayers are the beginning of your spiritual daily practice.

2. Set a time limit for each chapter (a week is a good suggested time limit), and do the chapter exercises in your journal. In this way you will become comfortable and familiar with the exercises, and can add them to your list of Spiritual Fitness practices. Some chapters contain more than one exercise and it is fine to spread them out over a longer period of time. It is best not to go on to further chapters until you have completed the exercises from the chapter you are reading. Some exercises that are done in one sitting can be refined and clarified by reviewing the exercise in your journal each day that week until you have modified it to the way you want it. For example, the *master plan* and *priority wheel* can be reconsidered, edited, and recomposed until they reflect you best. If you get busy and off track or are out of town for some time, just go back to your practices as soon as you are done. Do not criticize yourself for missing days, but honor and respect your commitment to make time for yourself and your growth. It is

the commitment to the program that is the key
to your success!

3. In each chapter, other books and tapes are recommended and a resource list is noted at the
end of the chapter. Explore some other information that you feel drawn to pursue. This is very
important. Note the book descriptions in the
text or titles from the resource list to which you
are attracted. Learn to pay attention to these
attractions. You will begin to notice that you are
drawn to certain topics and will begin to trust
your intuition. This trust will carry over into
other areas of your life. You may notice that you
feel drawn to say something or not say something at critical times, or that you know just how
you should structure your day. Many aspects of
your life will respond to this type of paying
attention to what you are drawn to do or say.

4. When you reach the end of the book, choose the
techniques and practices that you feel work best
for you. Do the techniques in your daily practice
that have worked for you. You may change techniques in your daily practice as you grow and
change. Pursue the areas of interest that you
are drawn to pursue. Recognize that sometimes
while we pursue one interest, we find something
else that is a much better fit. Know that the
process of growth and Spiritual Fitness lasts
for a lifetime. Be aware that your study and
practice will bring you into the full realization
of yourself and your life purpose.

5. Find others who are willing to enter the spiritual path with you. It would be useful to meet once a week or month with others using the Spiritual Fitness program. Another possibility is to find one other person to partner with on the journey. Sometimes people you already know will have similar interests and want to pursue Spiritual Fitness with you. You can support each other, share ideas, and discuss ways to bring Spiritual Fitness into your life, relationships, and work. If there is no one who may want to make the commitment at this time, it is certainly empowering to do it on your own. It will create strength of purpose and fuel your personal desire for a happier life through Spiritual Fitness.

At first, avoid conversations about your spiritual path with people who may oppose your choice to begin a spiritual practice. This protects your commitment from interference that can cause confusion early on the path. You would not try to explain to someone how to read or fish or pilot an airplane until you had finished the course, and the same is true for Spiritual Fitness. Once you are well grounded in your spiritual life, there will be time to discuss different ideas.

And so, let us begin.

1

Beginning the Path to Spiritual Fitness

The fruit of love is service, which is compassion in action. Religion has nothing to do with compassion; it is our love for God that is the main thing because we have all been created for the sole purpose to love and be loved.

—Mother Teresa, *For the Love of God*

Riches You Will Gain from This Chapter

- A decision to follow a spiritual path
- A commitment to heal your life through Spiritual Fitness
- A decision about where, if, and how religion has a place in your life
- An assessment of your current spiritual life
- The beginning of your daily practice
- A "brain map" of a past spiritual experience
- The discovery of the master plan for your life
- A belief in the master plan
- Priorities
- An assessment of your relationship to others, and to yourself, your body, your work, and your possessions

MY JOURNEY BEGAN THE day I knew that my spirit had touched someone hundreds of miles away with healing, and my journey toward Spiritual Fitness had begun. At the age of twenty-one, my life was profoundly and permanently changed. It was my first year as a special education teacher of learning disabled, emotionally disturbed, and hyperactive children. I had fifteen children ranging in age from six to twelve relying on me to break through their disabilities, to spark comprehension of all their academic subjects. No one had told me it could not be done and so in my energetic naivete, I took on the task and began to learn the meaning of stress. When the mother of one of my students suggested that I might benefit from a stress management class, I accepted her advice. She was a bit mysterious about the content of the class, only saying it had changed her life and might do the same for me. She had come to learn the meaning of stress trying to meet the demands of her charming, but severely reading disabled son.

I arrived early that Saturday morning for the stress management course in jeans and a long-sleeved lavender sweater, sipping coffee through a straw, prepared to spend the next two days learning to relax. What happened was another story with a much more moving and universal ending.

The class, which took place over the course of two full weekends, was based on the work of Jose Silva. Silva knew that when a person becomes calm, the brain waves indicate profound relaxation, allowing for greater use of their potential. He discovered that we could project our thoughts like a radar signal, gathering and delivering information that was normally unavailable to the conscious mind.

At first, we learned basic relaxation techniques and how to ask our minds to create dreams during the sleep state in order to solve problems. We accessed parts of the brain that would help to locate lost objects, and we learned to change our body temperatures. The body temperature exercise is the same one that is used when patients use biofeedback to medically treat health conditions. Biofeedback gives information about the body, such as temperature or brain wave activity to assist in knowing when the body is tense or relaxed.

In the second weekend, we learned to send our awareness to plants, objects, and animals in order to effectively pray for them. We gathered diagnostic information about their problems for the purpose of sending them healing energy and prayers. And if learning how to effectively pray was not enough, on the last afternoon of the last day of the last weekend of the program, we prepared to send our consciousness to the human body.

We studied diagrams of the skeletal system, the muscular system, the respiratory system, and the organs, with the intention of making it easier to visualize them and to render a healing to someone in need. We invited the healing by placing our focus directly on God or divine intelligence and allowing that intelligence to create changes in others' health. We allowed ourselves to be vessels for their healing by God.

We were then paired with a partner whom we did not know. Mine was a quiet man about twenty years my senior with salt-and-pepper hair. He wanted me to work on his mother as a case. As instructed, he told me only his mother's name, age, and city of origin. I went into meditation and there she was, on the mental screen of my mind. Rachel had short, curly gray hair and a wide mid-section. The veins in her legs were bulging and discolored, and her heart was enlarged. I knew that her weight was causing problems with her heart and legs and I even saw a lock on the refrigerator. I then prayed for her healing. When I came back to wakefulness after the meditation, I learned from Rachel's son that everything I had seen had been true. He had even told her that he would put a lock on the refrigerator to keep her from overeating. In that moment, I knew that consciousness has the freedom to move about, that our spirits are real and exist separate from our bodies, that they last eternally, and that we can send our spirits to heal and do good work.

I had been so profoundly impacted by that life-changing moment that I recognized the existence of

God in a whole new way. It was then that the path to Spiritual Fitness began. I began to learn how I could use my mind to change my limiting beliefs, heal old wounds, and help others to do the same. I hope that you will join me on the path, as we discover many different ways to reach the closest and most profound connection with your spirit, and God, possible.

DECIDING TO FOLLOW A SPIRITUAL PATH

For the sake of the people, for the sake of the planet, for the sake of the empowering presence of God in an increasingly godless world, we must search for God with all the new lights we have.

—Marcus Borg and Ross Mackenzie, *God at 2000*

MY JOURNEY BEGAN AT that stress management workshop when I learned that my spirit and good intentions could be used to tap into spiritual healing abilities, and profoundly and permanently changed my life. Our spirit, our soul, is the energy that feeds our hearts, minds, and bodies. Yet so many people are experiencing a poverty of health, love, clear thinking, and spiritual understanding that they are reading every self-help book they can find. Peter Russell reminds us that from the moment of our birth, our culture falsely encourages us to believe that outer well-being is the source of inner fulfillment (*Waking Up in Time*, 1992). While readers are devouring books on how to be beautiful and lose weight, how to manage their relationships, how to heal their hurts, raise their IQs and get promotions, they are "how-to-ing" themselves into debt. But few are getting the outcomes they so desperately desire. It is time to consider that the need is not to work harder, but to work differently. If you have any doubt that Spiritual Fitness is needed in your life, look at what you have accomplished without it. Is it everything you had hoped? If not, then strengthen your agreement with yourself to follow this path, now.

Why not become spiritually fit? Becoming spiritually fit does not mean that you should abandon your goals for personal achievement, health, wealth, or well being. It merely means that by putting your spirit first, all other things can be accomplished *and* maintained. The accomplishment of the goals is then completed in harmony with what is best for you and others, and not at the expense of what is best.

Alternatives to Spiritual Fitness have produced a multibillion-dollar weight-loss industry, yet Americans' body images suffer from continued comparison to society's accepted norms of fashion models' appearances. People are discouraged, overweight, anorexic, and bulimic. Working from the outside in has not made the desperately desired difference.

In most lives, there is a sense of striving, of longing for something, a sense of incompleteness. People try to fill the need with relationships, money, sex, power, busyness, business, chaos, confusion, clutter, food, alcohol, drugs, or any other addiction that makes the longing go away for a brief time. This tail-chasing is often like running around in the circle surrounding a hole in order to avoid falling in the hole. Sometimes we are avoiding what we might find by going deeper into ourselves.

How about starting at the very inner core, with your spirit, to become fit? Learning how to feel the fullness of your own spirit, rather than stifle it by society's programming about who you should be, may end the hunger by filling it with inner peace. Peace does not separate us from our goals, but allows us to get in touch with who we truly are, and to attain our goals in a way that is right for us. Peace allows us to heal and become empowered in a true sense. Spiritual Fitness can guide you toward a fulfilling, enriching life for the duration, not just while you break an addiction, do aerobics, spice up a love life, or heal a broken heart.

When we truly find our connection with our spirit, we might not be completely cured of our need to run and hide, and our lives will certainly not be perfect, but we will be well on our way to working through and understanding what we are running from, and what other possibilities exist. It is kind of like polishing the facets of a diamond. The more we work at it, the more facets we have and the more brightly we can shine. The more we recognize our spirituality, the more we polish our facets. Our connection with our spirit is the only thing we can never lose. It already exists, waiting for us to discover it.

Often, our longing for things is unconsciously connected with the longing to be closer to our own spirituality. By beginning to follow our spiritual purpose, we begin to release the incompleteness we feel and the need for substitutions subsides. Once this gap is filled with our sense of spirit, a sense of inner peace takes over, replacing the need to fill what used to be a void. We are then on the spiritual path, so to speak.

In examining your longing, part of you may be asking, "What is my life or soul purpose in being here?" and, "How do I fulfill that purpose?" These are important questions and the search for answers generally moves us in the right direction—toward the discovery of our life plan. While there may be a sense of frustration that comes from longing in a personal sense, each step that your awakened spirit takes on the path moves you further toward the fulfillment of your purpose. Follow your instincts, for they are what brought you to this book.

Many spiritual paths can lead to Spiritual Fitness. In order to achieve it, begin with the truth that there *is* a God. Many people, because of negative past experience, do not even like the use of the word "God." They may feel that the word "God" represents an elusive being or a patriarchal monarch. Do not get caught up in terminology. We are talking about the spiritual life force of which you are a part. You may choose to use a new term to describe the infinite deity. Master, divine master, universal intelligence, or some other terminology may be needed for you to reframe a previously negative concept of a God.

It is good to stand on as many sides of God as you can, to see God through the eyes of Moses and Abraham, the Dalai Lama, Jesus, Paramahansa Yogananda, Mohammed, Confucius, and any others you feel attracted to examine. Religion is a path to spiritual transformation. All religious paths lead to the same central point, but because they all come from different directions, the scenery differs. Each describes the view of God as it appears from their road map, much like travelers coming from around the world. Each description of the path is a reflection of the places each different traveler passes through on the way to some final destination. This is evident in the meditation practice of each religion. While the techniques differ, we all end up at the same center of silence and communication with God. Each provides a glimpse into the truth; each is a finger that points the way to the truth while none holds the entire truth. As you deepen your look at God through the various paths, you may experience greatly desired changes.

I share my own personal experiences, which provided me with knowledge and verification about the existence of God. I reveal a path through which you can find your own reality or presence of God, and put your own life on the path to self-fulfillment. You may already be aware that a God exists, and you may have a great deal of faith, either generally or as a member of an organized religion. It is important to recognize whether these beliefs are assisting your understanding of God or hindering it. Retain what helps, and let hindrances fall away. In either case, Spiritual Fitness will enrich your present vision.

In this knowing of the existence of God, we have a great understanding of ourselves that goes beyond our ability to be happy through the healing of our minds, bodies, or emotions in isolation. For example, a surgery may eliminate a physical growth, but will not change the relationship that we have with our bodies. In the long run, changing that relationship would enable us to better maintain our health and well being. If obtaining Spiritual Fitness does not improve physical health, then it will improve your awareness and understanding of health problems which will certainly create changes in how you take care of your physical self. Our minds, bodies, and emotions are the tools through which our spiritual understanding flows.

Exercise: Making a Commitment

Goal: Making a conscious commitment to heal your life through Spiritual Fitness.

If you are ready, now would be a good time to make your commitment to the spiritual path. Once you have done so, it is time to move on to examine your past experience and decide what you will keep on your path to Spiritual Fitness.

1. Say to yourself that you are committed.

2. Make your positive affirmation of commitment in your journal. Make today your first entry. Write down your thoughts on the decision you have made, and move on to the first exploration on the path.

RELIGION AND SPIRITUALITY

God . . . undying light in darkness, eternal limit-lessness, common consciousness in all creation . . . greater than doctrines or denominations, who calls me beyond and out of my limits.

—Joan D. Chittister, Marcus Borg, and
Ross Mackenzie, *God at 2000*

WHETHER YOU HAVE FELT a loss of your strength of spirit or never felt the presence of your spirit at all, the path of Spiritual Fitness will lead you to it. When I began to attend Catholic school in the first grade, much of my time was spent in church. I felt comfortable and at home there. I could often feel a presence filling me and the entire structure. It was the same sense of spirit I felt in my early years of life, yet it had expanded now. I had a name for what I felt inside, which was so strongly pro-voked in church—God. I was often moved to tears by the beauty of the choir in praising His/Her name. Church soon became a place I went just to be or to pray or to feel the presence of God. Even after attending morning services, I often put on my chapel veil (a requirement of the time), and my empire waist cotton dress, and walked back to church. I felt the presence of God early in life and I felt it in the churches of many religions, in nature, and in other people. It would only grow stronger with each passing year. At times in my life, when material matters became too important to me, I lost my sense of connection to God. At these times I found that attempting to reach goals separate from spirit was only self-defeating. I worked harder than I needed to accomplish goals and experienced losses. My desire to regain that connection propelled me forward on the path to Spiritual Fitness. I learned that at the times when I felt distant from God, I had been the one who had moved away.

In the Catholic Church, I found, at that time, a powerful and full acceptance of guardian angels and saints. I knew there were many different spiritual assistants I could call upon to guide me on my path. The church background provided a spiritual foundation, which would beckon me many times on my path. I knew I benefited from the church teachings and accepted many of their truths. I then began an intense comparative study of other religions to expand my knowledge and understanding of divine intelligence. I realized that organized religion tended to say God was just one thing or another, but not that God was everything.

In Christianity and Judaism, the major religions of the Western world, I noted that you had to be Jewish or Christian in order to be assured a place in heaven. Each religion taught that we must follow with specific practices in order to be properly praising God. It seemed they could not all be learned simultaneously and that each, in their own way, had tried to limit, make finite, or dogmatize an entity that was infinite and unobtainable. Yet, in our human need for understanding, we attempted to put limits and names on God in order to make Divine Intelligence our own. We each wanted to feel special and to have rules to live by so that we would all know that we were doing it correctly.

RELIGION'S ROLE ON THE PATH TO SPIRITUAL FITNESS

First God created us and then we created God.

—Marcus Borg and Ross Mackenzie, *God at 2000*

I NEEDED TO LET go of some of these manmade teachings because they could only limit my growth. As a first step toward Spiritual Fitness, you will need to take stock of the awarenesses of past teachings about your spiritual life, teachings which you have accepted until now. It will be time to "clean house" as you decide for yourself which teachings clearly connect you to your spirit and which ones separate you from your spirit. Moving from the limits and rules into the infinite is a life-long journey. You will encounter your fears of letting go, as you would with many lifetime goals. The journey has given me proof that, indeed, there is a God, that there are angels and helper spirits, that there is life after death, and that we can cross back and forth into these dimensions.

Prior to his death, psychologist Carl Jung was asked, "Do you believe in God?" He answered, "No, I know there is a God. Belief suggests a theory ... I know." In his statement he presents the reality of the existence of God which is essential to our fulfillment and is more real than what we tangibly consider to be reality. Anyone can accomplish the same life changing awareness of the existence of God, of life after death, of the spirit or soul as a place where our own God awareness resides. Anyone can be on the path to a fulfilling and rewarding life.

LOOKING BACK TO WHERE YOU'VE BEEN TO SEE WHERE YOU'RE GOING

The past does not equal the future.

—Cheatwood Research Institute

A *SPIRITUAL ASSESSMENT* IS one of the first tools on the path to Spiritual Fitness. In a *spiritual assessment* you must look at the spiritual influences, or lack of them, that you have had prior to this time. Usually past religious experiences will be part of your assessment. You may find, through the assessment and future study, that you can be open to a true sense of God's infinity by following certain religious practices that you have learned. You may instead choose from other religions' practices or develop your own practices. The idea is to first identify the influence of your past religious experience. You may find religion is one path to Spiritual Fitness for you. All paths lead to the same central point.

Most of us have had some religious experience in our lives, good, bad, or indifferent. These experiences may have led us closer, or further away from spiritual understanding. Many people tell me that they disliked their early experiences or found their spiritual elders to be lacking in compassion. We will examine the effects of those experiences in the next exercise.

Every major religion holds a piece of the truth of God and yet the whole is greater than the individual parts. Each conceptualizes God in a different way, historically. With Judaism, the concept of one central God, known as Yahweh, began the belief that Jews were God's chosen people suggesting a special relationship with Him. In that relationship, they are required to act as witnesses to his goodness. Abraham was the founder of Judaism.

Jesus Christ, our Savior, was a Jew. While he did not change the original Jewish laws, he added the law of love. He established the Christian church, including Catholicism and Protestantism. Jesus' focus was on the spirit as the most important commodity in life. In the Bible in the book of Mark, Jesus says, "For what shall it profit man, if he shall gain the whole world and lose his own soul?" Even Jesus Christ had to let go of his ego and accept the path of his higher self by accepting the crucifixion. This religion says that we can transcend our daily experiences through faith.

Christianity differs from other religions in that it sees God as a trinity: Father, Son, and Holy Spirit. Based on religious principles, man is usually considered a duality.

The Aztecs in Mexico and Peru were highly developed civilizations as early as the sixteenth century. The beautiful Incan city of Machu Picchu was one of their great contributions to the world. In these religious cultures, sacrifices to the gods were common. These early cultures had different gods instead of one deity.

The Islamic religion, one of the oldest in existence, was founded by Muhammad. His religion united the Arab nations. The prophet received revelations from a messenger, later identified as Angel Gabriel, that were written down in the Koran, the sacred book of Islam. This religion, differing from the Judeo-Christian tradition, directed not only one's relationship with God, but also social and political matters. Muhammed became the example of virtuous character for millions of Islamic people.

The Buddhist religion was founded by Siddhartha Gautama, the Buddha. He attained a state of mystical contemplation, which later formed the basis for the modern practice of Buddhist meditation. It is a peaceful religion, based on social equality and a belief that man's freedom from suffering comes from freedom from selfish desires. A broad definition of health is embraced that includes the health of the whole person. Buddhist meditation allows for mystical experiences, which free the mind from psychological states of fear, superiority and inferiority, insecurity and doubt, and egotism. When I studied and participated in their practices, I experienced a sense of freedom from attachment that was instrumental in my growth.

The oldest spiritual tradition is shamanism. It was an early attempt to connect with God by leaving ordinary reality to journey into the higher realms. In these realms, shamans would assist in healing the sick and acquiring spiritual powers. By helping others the shaman achieves more self-fulfillment and spiritual power, transcending self-centeredness. Freedom from self-centeredness is a major step in mental and emotional health and self-awareness.

Once I realized that each major religion had a partial view of infinite intelligence, I explored how each contributed to the whole. I began to participate in the ceremonies of different religions, gaining from them a partial view of the infinite. As a part of this research I experienced a miraculous process while attending a mass in a charismatic church. While attending the service, one of the parishioners, a man known to be rather egotistical, had the awareness that we have a higher purpose than that of gratifying the ego. He wanted to begin living from his higher self within the *master plan*. He asked permission to approach the altar, prostrated himself in front of it, and kissed the ground. As sometimes happens on the spiritual path, I experienced a mental image. I saw, in my mind, a large crucifix overtop of the man and was moved to tears. Apparently, the priest saw the same image, for he began to weep also and describe his vision. He told the congregation that there was rejoicing in heaven because the man had just crucified his personality and opened himself to the *master plan* of his spirit. The priest's words verified the image that I had seen. You may begin to receive these verifications also, once you begin to follow a spiritual path.

The surrender of the ego is the dawning of the truth that we are spiritual beings living a physical life. Tests may occur, problems may still exist, and others may try to draw you back into an old way of life, but all of these issues can be resolved spiritually. You may face rejection from others who resent you for rising above old patterns. This occurs any time that there is a growth process of any kind, so do not be afraid. These experiences will be replaced with something better, or friends may even decide to change and join you on the path.

Tests take many forms and are often self-created, but the more we pass them, the more we move along on the spiritual path to life fitness. We give up much of the unhappiness created by our illusions. We may not know the depth of why things are the way they are, but once we have a sense of what direction to take, destinations will find us. Money, power, happiness, wealth, and approval may elude us if we pursue them from our egos, but these things may come to us if they are part of our life purpose and we are living from our spirit. Richard Bach's book *Illusions* illustrates this concept in an honest and entertaining way and is an excellent reference for the study of this truth.

Exercise: Spiritual Assessment—Part I

Goal: Defining the role of religion in your life.

In your journal answer the following questions:

1. What is your earliest memory of a spiritual or religious experience?

2. What is your best memory of a spiritual or religious experience?

3. What is your worst memory of a spiritual or religious experience?

List your worst recollections of a religious experience in the column on the left. In the right column, list the person or manmade law or circumstance that was responsible for the negative experience.

Memory   **Cause**

_____   _____

_____   _____

_____   _____

_____   _____

_____   _____

_____   _____

_____   _____

Now answer the following questions.

4. When have you felt closest to your sense of God/divine master from a religious experience?

5. When have you felt closest to God outside of a religious experience (examples: at the ocean, at the birth of a baby, picking flowers, playing guitar, etc.)

6. What do you feel your past religious experience has taught you that you would like to hold onto and continue to incorporate into your life?

First, let's examine the unpleasant memories and the situation or person responsible for them. In this way, you can separate God from these unpleasant memories. Generally, they are created by those around us and make it unpleasant for us to feel a connection to God. It may be necessary to do some healing around these memories in order to separate your awareness of God from the past negative memory. There will be techniques discussed later in the book which can assist in making these changes. Again, it may be necessary for you to make these changes with professional guidance if they were traumatic or deeply embedded.

Next, let's examine the past religious experiences you would like to keep. Perhaps it was your bar mitzvah party or communion service, your marriage service, or a beautiful and touching funeral ceremony. Religions, whether formal or informal, organize rituals and ceremonies, which are often joyous occasions attended by family and friends. Rituals and ceremonies in your life may be important to continue. If so, find ways to create them in your own life. A friend's mother recently finalized her divorce by completing a Native American ritual of spending a day in the woods releasing her past. Ritual may be something that you can use to constructively channel spiritual experiences—whatever your positive experiences of ritual or ceremony were.

Exercise: Spiritual Assessment—Part II

Goal: Putting religion in the right place for you.

1. In deciding what to keep from past experience, think of ways you can include good memories in your life.

2. It may be useful to complete a brain map. Start with a topic in the center. Allow yourself to list around it all of the ideas that remind you of the topic in the center. Don't filter out any ideas at this stage, just let them flow. Choose a spiritual memory that was positive for you and write it in the center of the circle on the brain map. In the example below the memory is Sabbath services. If you have enjoyed attending Sabbath services, you might want to work with that as follows:

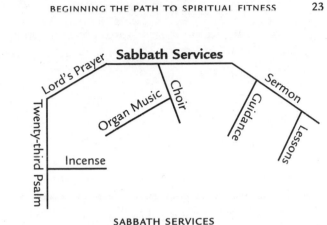

SABBATH SERVICES

In this manner, you can see which aspects of the experiences you want to keep. Use as many lines as you want, putting related ideas under one another.

3. Then, list in your journal ways and times to include these things in your life in the present. Schedule one on your appointment calendar now. Then move on to the next exercise.

Daily Practice

These statements are prayers and can be a perfect way to begin your path to Spiritual Fitness. Daily practices are one of the best ways to bring Spiritual Fitness into your life. Start any *daily practice* with the prayer statement that you will identify next. This will be the first element of your *daily practice*, one that you will add to as you continue on your spiritual path. Keep your statement with you. Take it out and read it anytime you lose sight of your faith.

Exercise: Discovering Your Prayer Statement

Goal: Connecting to God through past experiences.

1. Think of the time you felt closest to God. Relive that experience now. Close your eyes and remember what you could see at the time. Recall everything you could hear, maybe even things you hadn't paid attention to at the time. Notice what you felt, emotionally and physically. Where in your body did you feel the connection to God? What in your life now reminds you of this feeling?

2. Create a brief prayer or phrase to remind you of this experience. Examples: "Thank God for breathing life into my daughter's tiny body. She is my joy every day," or "I will never forget picking vegetables I planted in my garden, marveling at how a tiny seed grew to provide food for my life."

3. Make this statement something that you remind yourself of daily during a specified time that is set aside for *daily practice*.

When I began to think about what made me feel close to God, I was reminded of the most profound and life-changing experience I had during the first meditation class I had taken based on the work of Jose Silva.

Feeling that my spirit had touched someone hundreds of miles away with healing began my journey to Spiritual Fitness. From that experience, I knew it was necessary to bring meditation into my life. I did a brain map to see what all of the things were that I associated with meditation. The map looked something like this:

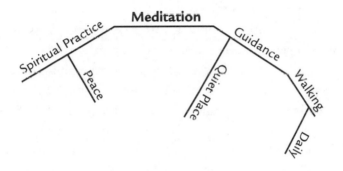

MEDITATION

After doing this map, I wrote the prayer statement, "My first meditation brought me closer to God." Reading this statement became the first step in my *daily practice*. I then studied many forms of meditation that I have incorporated, not only as a *daily practice*, but as ongoing "walking meditation." This means being in a state of receptivity that guides us through our days, weeks, months, years, and lives. This acceptance of guidance and openness and receptivity to guidance is part of walking on the path of our *master plan*.

Another consideration in putting negative experiences into perspective and turning your attention to

positive ones is this: although they may have been
created through the behavior of someone's misun-
derstanding of God, or a manmade law, it may be
possible that these negative experiences caused us to
change in some way that later became positive. Did
they cause you to change your life direction, did they
cause you to abandon parts of your past, and did they
strengthen you or prepare you in some way for activities of the future? Did you suffer financially, causing
you to become a better manager of money?

Look at the ways in which negative experiences have
changed your life, attitudes, or life direction. If those
experiences simply caused you bitterness and did not
benefit you in any way, perhaps the lesson to be learned
is one of healing the self and forgiving others. Forgiveness in one of the most powerful forces in the universe.
It can release old pain and create change. One of the
changes it can make is to free up all the mental energy
we use holding onto old pain. Even if we never think of
the issue, part of the subconscious is overwhelmed
with the task of holding old anger. It uses up more
energy than you may realize to hold anger. Just imagine how much energy it would take for you to constantly hold something in your hand or carry it in a
bag thrown over your shoulder. Holding information
in the subconscious is much the same. Once a negative
emotion is released, you may experience a noticeable
increase in your physical and emotional energy.

Once forgiveness has been made to those in the past,
the future can change and be transformed. The act of

forgiveness releases a power that cleans the slate of our past, lets go of our wounds, and gives us power to move on. Without forgiveness, our lives may be identified by our wounds, and we may cling to them in order to control others. We may say, for example, that because we had an abusive situation in our past, that we are no longer able to trust anyone, and then we make others jump through hoops in order to gain our trust. Isn't this a way of maintaining power by refusing to forgive? Forgiveness frees us to be able to react and respond in the present moment, rather than from reacting out of past wounds. It clears the static from our vision and allows us to see what truly is, rather than what we imagine is true based on old wounds. The techniques in chapter 2 are especially useful for healing the pain of our past. A review of these techniques will lead you to understand how you can assist in healing your own past. Again, for traumatic memories, be sure to seek the assistance of a professional in your healing process.

SPIRITUAL MASTER PLAN

What lies behind us and what lies before us are
tiny matters, compared to what lies within us.

—Ralph Waldo Emerson

THE SPIRITUAL *MASTER PLAN* is the idea behind all of our creation. Without it, our blueprints could not be drawn by our mind and our emotional wiring could not respond to our blueprint. Our bodies are our reflections of the operation of our understanding of the *master plan*. As in the construction of a home, the great unseen *master plan* must exist. This is why houses in our dreams, imaginations, or lives are such strong reflections of who we are. Metaphorically speaking, the house represents the self, or our comprehension of who we are in the *master plan*. Our being is much like a house. A house requires a plan, a blueprint, joists, wiring, walls, furnishings, and a yard. Without the plan or spirit of the house, the house could not be brought into being. Our physical houses are the result of our comprehension of the *master plan*, which reflects our level of awareness of our spirit. Our goal is to use the metaphor of a house to help discover our *master plan*.

The components of the *master plan* include:

- Mental Blueprint
- Emotional Wiring
- Physical Joists
- Manifestation Garden

Once we put our spirit in charge and become receptive, we begin to receive signals from the spirit or master that allow us to set up the blueprint. We receive mental inspiration about how our life blueprint should look. This mental blueprint is a reflection of the way in which our lives need to be constructed at the time. Leaving the *master plan* in charge of the blueprint helps get the ego out of the way. In so doing you can be assured that you are serving your highest purpose in life rather than just your personal desires. While the *master plan* needs the ego to work through and the mind to create awareness of the plan, the ego should not be in the driver's seat. Ego-driven lives are often fear-driven and lack the contentment of the spiritually driven life.

How can you determine when your life is ego driven? It may happen if you become too materialistic and possessions cause you to lose sight of what is truly important. Or maybe your personal desires push out the needs of those who care about you. Sometimes, just looking at the outcome you are working toward can show you if they are ego driven. Will the outcome benefit you and others or will it benefit you to the detriment of others? At times, when we don't want to do what others want us to do, it is a lesson for them to learn. Others may need to see that trying to control us to suit themselves is inappropriate. If, on the other hand, the work we have to do for ourselves is also the same work that we need to do to be in right relationship to others, we are usually on the right track in our *master plan*.

The first goal in the *master plan* is to draw the blueprint. We put up the physical structure of the house. These joists are comparable to our physical body structure and its relationship to our mind, emotions, and spirit. If the mind is in close contact with the plan, the body functions accordingly and carries out the purpose of the plan. Physical dysfunctions may come from issues of false ego or pride or even from life's fears. On the other hand, sometimes physical dysfunctions are part of the working out of the plan. This working out may include the clearing of some old beliefs that are physically manifested in the body in order to be more visible. Making them visible makes it possible for them to be reconsidered, understood, and revised or discarded. This concept will be addressed more completely later as we examine the role of illness in setting priorities.

Our emotions are like the wiring that goes through the entire house, responding to the impulses and signals in our lives. They are our feeling responses to our awareness of our thoughts and spiritual inspirations. They include our desires and attractions for various life paths or courses of action. Our responses to the world also are evidenced here. The gardens we create represent the physical manifestations of the creative action of our spirit, mind, body, and emotions. Gardens are the outcomes of our willingness to put all parts of ourselves into creating our world.

The degree to which we can conceive of the *master plan* is the degree to which we can see how we are spiritual beings with a soul purpose. That purpose drives our mind, body, and emotions to allow the plan to work itself through and construct our lives. There are small sparks of the infinite, ready to sparkle, once we have an idea of how we can best do so.

Biblically speaking, we are made in His/Her image and likeness as small expressions of something greater.

Our flow in life, our degree of acceptance and understanding of life, and eventually our happiness in life, are
reflections of our connection to the *master plan*. Once we
are aware of our connection, we are fully on the path to
spiritual and personal fulfillment. Our finances, relationships, looks, health, friends, accomplishments, and
possessions—while reflections of our self-image—are
temporary. While they are tangible, we cannot rely only
on them. Tangibles can all be lost in a moment. On the
other hand, we cannot lose our spirit. It lasts because
our true nature is spiritual.

It is crucial to remember to keep our spiritual
understanding of ourselves in charge and to remember
that our spirit is the source of the *master plan* behind
our creations and manifestations. Who we think we
are is mostly a manifestation of our personality, and
who others think we are is often a reflection of who
they need for us to be. Even love, when it is simply a
reflection of the human ego, is sometimes a reflection
of ourselves by another person in the way they need to
see us at the time. What we need, think we need, and
what the other person needs can change, and so love,
driven by the ego, can change, too. The *master plan* does
not change. It may, in fact, lead you to a soul partner
who is matched to your path, rather than an illusion-
ary relationship which manifests only the personality.

Exercise: Priority Wheel

Goal: To set your Spiritual Fitness priorities. Draw a priority wheel like the below in your journal:

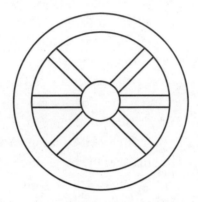

PRIORITY WHEEL

1. Be as honest as you can with yourself as you decide where to place your priorities on the wheel. What do you put at the center of your priorities? Is it family, or making a living, or appearance? Write that in the center of the wheel.

2. Then place your other priorities on the spokes of the wheel.

3. Look at the center priority. How does it effect all the other priorities? Write your answer in your journal.

4. Now draw another wheel. This time place your spirit in the center. Then place the other priorities on the spokes of the wheel. Think about how

the other priorities are effected by the central
spiritual priority. You may notice how the central
priority governs the way you relate to all other
priorities. Write your ideas about how placing
your spiritual life at the center changes your relationship to other priorities.

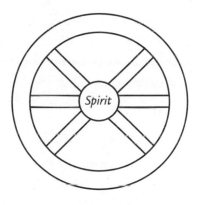

Once your relationship to yourself and your spirit
are aligned, your life follows suit. Your priorities are
not necessarily designed to fit in with your spirit, but
instead to revolve around it. The fact that your spirit
existed before you did and exists after you are gone
allows you to see how your spirit is the eternal. Try letting your eternal spirit be the guiding force in your
Spiritual Fitness.

When you think about a wheel, if it was not for the
space in the middle, the wheel would have no use. The
spokes would merely collide into one another and the
wheel would not turn. Our lives are much the same.
Without the spirit in the center, our lives get stuck,
and do not roll forward.

Maintaining a right relationship to God allows you to maintain a balance in yourself. That centers you and helps you keep your feet on the ground in any situation. If the first priority in your life is your spirituality and your relationship with Divine Mind, then it will be at the center of your priorities wheel. Everything else will work in conjunction with your first priority. If you are meditating, clearing old mental programs, and keeping your spirit at the heart of your life, then other priorities begin to revolve around the spiritual center.

THE PRIORITY WHEEL AND YOUR HEALTH

From counseling to acupuncture, to every level of bodywork, such as massage, to meditation and visualization—are all focused on assisting the patient in releasing the very stresses that are causing the destruction of the physical body.

—Carolyn Myss, *The Creation of Health*

HOW DOES MAINTAINING YOUR health serve a spiritual purpose? Keeping a high level of health and energy in the body provides a good home for the spirit. It gives us a vehicle in which to live that expresses our highest expression of our spirit.

All of your thoughts produce a reaction in the body, either for good or harm. First, practically speaking, when your priority is your spirit, you can worry less. You can accept that your life is in divine order and that you will be led to follow the spiritual *master plan* for your life. That one act of faith alleviates stress, the greatest destroyer of health. Stress causes rapid shallow breathing that robs your cells of oxygen. The cells, lacking in the fuel that they need, become weak and the immune system becomes weakened. Stress strains the heart, endocrine system and most other systems of the body causing a host of diseases. Among them are heart disease, diabetes, and hypothyroidism and adrenal function.

Take a position in which you avoid self-criticism and judgement. You wouldn't treat your best friend judgmentally. Treat yourself with the same care you would a best friend. Become nurturing and caring. Avoid self-blame. If something goes wrong, just ask yourself what you can do better next time. Write about it in your journal.

By maintaining a position of faith, with your spirit at the center of your priorities, fear, doubt, and anxiety are diminished. You can accept that you are committed to uplifting your life and that life circumstances are part of the path. As you accept your life and see how you can use Spiritual Fitness to make it better, you will struggle less and avoid unnecessary blame and guilt, and the stress they cause on the body.

Take an attitude of "beginner's mind" (Kabat-Zinn, *Mindfulness Meditation*). In doing so you allow yourself to see everything as if for the first time. This frees you from old patterns of judgement, opening you to be receptive to new possibilities. By living in the moment you are not regretting the past or worrying about the future. By doing so, you relieve the body of a great deal of wear and tear as it responds to the thoughts of the mind.

Specific health problems have been linked to specific attitudes (Louise L. Hay's *Heal Your Body*). For example, if you are a rigid thinker, unable to take in new ideas, you may hold your body in a rigid position. Over time, that creates muscle tension and even arthritis. Other people who are chronic worriers know that their stomachs become highly reactive to their thoughts and experience digestive problems. The relationship between mind and body is a complex and profound one. It is primarily in western society that the two have been treated as if they are separate.

Exercise: Assessment of Your Health

Now look at the expectations you have accepted from others about your physical body. Are you expected to live up to responsibilities that are beyond your physical capabilities? If so, as you strive too hard, you create stress and illness. Look at the expectations of others that you have internalized and accepted. Do you feel you have to live up to the role models of physical appearance that have been set by the culture? Do you feel you must conform to be accepted by peers, colleagues, and family? If so, reexamine what you have taken into your own belief system. Separate from these beliefs by asking yourself, What do I want for my physical self? What is the level of

health and appearance that I want? Then ask yourself what level of health most supports your personal and Spiritual Fitness goals. How can you manage your health in a way that supports your spiritual
purpose? How do you best reflect a glowing inner
spirit and feelings of spiritual self-love? Certainly
not by being overly demanding and wearing yourself
out. Spiritual Fitness is well reflected by self care.

For example, exercise keeps you healthy and energetic so that you can fulfill your spiritual life. However, exercising too much is a form of self-punish-
ment that works against self love.

If you could regain all of the mental energy you have
spent worrying about appearances, you could use it
to change your world. Take back your energy now.
Make decisions about what is best for your health
and body. Stop worrying about this part of your life
and follow a plan for health. Stick to your decisions.
If you find that you can't keep these decisions, they
may not be right for you, or you may have wounds
in your self-esteem that keep you from taking care
of yourself.

Many of the practices to follow will help you to heal
these wounds so that you can care for yourself. The
breathing practices will interrupt the stress response
created by worry and negative thinking. You can then
release your thoughts with the breath, freeing your
body from a stressful response. The mind watching
exercise you will learn later will give you a tool to help

release thoughts that are harmful to the body. Following that, the practice of visualization will show you how to heal by seeing yourself well. You are your primary healer.

THE PRIORITY WHEEL AND RELATIONSHIPS

> An unreserved positive self-adoration remains the essence of health, the most important asset a patient must gain to become exceptional. Self-esteem and self love are not sinful. They make living a joy instead of a chore.
>
> —Bernie Siegel, *Love, Medicine and Miracles*

WHAT ABOUT RELATIONSHIPS? YOUR relationships with others are often a reflection of your relationship with yourself. When you love and respect yourself, you expect others to do the same. This sets up an expectation that you will be treated positively. Positive expectation is one of the greatest enhancements to relationships.

When you adopt a spiritual path, you feel better about yourself and have a sense of empowerment. This increases self-love, which leads to the positive expectation that others will like you and treat you well. If they don't, you don't take it personally. You realize that their mistreatment may have to do with them and not you.

Dean Ornish, in *Love and Survival*, speaks of the physical healing benefits of loving relationships. One

of the Swedish studies he cites showed that the avail-
ability of deep emotional relationships was associated
with less coronary artery blockage. Researchers have
found that the quality of relationships is the deciding
factor in health benefit, rather than the quantity of
relationships. "Anything that promotes feelings of love
and intimacy is healing; anything that promotes isolation, separation, loneliness, loss . . . often leads to suffering, disease, and premature death from all causes."

Forgiveness is a theme that I will raise in various
contexts. I do so because it is so central to Spiritual
Fitness, especially to emotional fitness. When you can
forgive yourself, you can take responsibility for your
actions. Many people cannot forgive themselves, so
they live in denial. They do not admit that they did
anything wrong or hurt anyone. Their self-love is not
great enough to allow them to see their faults and
maintain self-love at the same time. If you can love
and accept your strengths and flaws, you can love the
lessons they provide. They are a part of the journey of
your life.

Once you accept and forgive yourself, you are then
less likely to make the same mistake again. You can
acknowledge your mistake to Divine Intelligence, make
amends where possible and learn the lesson from your
experience. Then see your strengths and love yourself.
Don't let a bad experience or behavior cause you to lose
self-love.

The same is true in your relationships with others.
Once you have begun to follow the spiritual path, you

have that commitment to feel good about. You can feel better about that commitment than any other while keeping it at the hub of your *priority wheel*. Your self-esteem is raised, your awareness of your spirit expands, and you can have more positive relationships with others. You are giving life your best so you can expect to get the best in return. Once you have learned to forgive yourself, you can learn to forgive others. As you become clearer in your self-perception and heal yourself of old pain, you can see others more clearly. You then make better choices about which people you accept into your life. When you are confident that you can make better choices, you stop isolating yourself from other people in order to avoid pain. By making that change, you can reap the health benefits that Dr. Ornish has described.

In choosing others, make sure they allow you to be your true spiritual self. True relationships foster honesty and integrity about who you are, rather than expecting you to be someone else.

Exercise: Assessment of Your Relationships

Goal: To clearly view your beliefs about others

1. List the expectations you have about others in your journal. Do you expect people to be loving and friendly and to like you? Do you believe that people want the best for you? Or do you think that people are rejecting and will deny

you what you want and need. Look at the
beliefs you have about others. They are most
likely what you will experience.

2. Now look at your list of expectations. If they are
positive keep them. You will usually experience a
positive outcome with others. When you do not,
realize that their behavior is about their self perception not yours. If you have written negative
beliefs, write the reverse of the belief. For example, if the negative belief is that others will deny
you what you need, rephrase it. Write down that
other people recognize my needs and respond to
them. If you think that people are rude, restate
it in the positive. Write that others are kind and
considerate toward you. Add these positive affirmations to your *daily practice* after your God
statement.

3. For the second part of this exercise, identify the
past experience that began the negative perception. Notice what happened in your life that
formed the belief. If you have had bad experiences with others that have formed perceptions
of harm, it is time to heal those perceptions. If
the events were traumatic and deeply harmful,
seek the help of a counselor with a spiritual ori-
entation to help you heal from them. If they were
typical events of growth and change, you may
want to work with them in the section on trance
breaking.

THE PRIORITY WHEEL AND POSSESSIONS

> . . . our addiction to materialism. We are trying to
> make ourselves feel better. But any happiness we
> get is usually only temporary; as soon as one
> "high" wears off, we go in search of another "fix."
>
> —Peter Russell, *Waking Up in Time*

LET'S LOOK AT POSSESSIONS. How do they express you in
the highest possible way? Are you chained to heavy
responsibilities of maintaining cars and homes? Does
that take your focus off of your spiritual expression?
Or do your possessions make it possible for you to
express your true self? Perhaps they provide a sense of
order and beauty that assists you in expressing your
highest self.

Materialism is a fact of life in Western society. Everywhere you are bombarded by a set of values that says
you should buy things in order to feel good about
yourself. In other societies this is not true or is true to a
lesser degree. Therefore, it is not a universal value, it is
just a belief that we have incorporated into our thinking through experience. Those beliefs can be changed.
Answer the following questions in your journal.

Exercise: Assessment of Material Wealth

Goal: To examine your relationships to possessions.

1. Ask yourself how you feel upon awakening first
   thing in the morning. What is your first experi-

ence before you have had a chance to view any material possessions?

2. Assess how you feel upon awakening versus how you feel after beginning involvement with material things. If you feel positive and emotionally balanced, then you are balanced. If you wake up feeling badly or pessimistic about yourself, notice whether you use material possessions to feel better about yourself. Do you rely on your car, your house, or the social prestige they bring to feel better about yourself?

Reliance on material things to feel better is a temporary fix. It makes you feel better briefly. But you need more and more physical possessions to feel better, because it is temporary. You always need another better car or house. It is good to enjoy your possessions and appreciate the work you did to obtain them, as long as they are not the cause of your happiness. Since material things can be lost in an instant, you can lose your happiness. If you are happy with who you are and know that your true identity is spiritual, you know that you can never lose that.

If material dependence is a pattern in which you find yourself, continue on the path of Spiritual Fitness. Change the hub of your *priority wheel*. Redirect your time, energy, and money. Begin *daily practices*.

If instead you wake up with positive emotions about yourself and find that external possessions only add to your existing well-being, then you may be approaching materialism in a balanced way. Possessions can even enhance Spiritual Fitness, when used in positive ways. Books and tapes assist in your growth. Cars get you to work and out to fulfill your spiritual purpose and connect with others. In this way, spirituality is the reason for those things and stays at the hub of your wheel.

THE PRIORITY WHEEL AND WORK

God does not demand of us that we walk another person's path. We are only asked to fulfill our own unique calling, becoming the person we are truly meant to be.

—Drew Leider, *Spiritual Passages*

WORK IS OFTEN AN area in which people can earn success in external ways, but without creating inner fulfillment and peace. There is always a need for another promotion, another raise, and another accolade. It may be possible that you are meeting many spiritual needs by working and moving forward, and are fulfilling your life purpose. But often this not the case. The attention to work is a way of gaining self-esteem by appearing more successful to others. If you are working for personal and spiritual satisfaction, you are probably in a right relationship with work. If it is a status symbol, however, look again. You may be using an addictive attitude to run from yourself and from true fulfillment.

Work is an area where many people are challenged to maintain a spiritual focus. Write your answers to the following questions in your journal. It will help you to put work in balance in your life.

Exercise: Assessment of Work

Goal: To understand your relationship with work.

1. Answer the following questions in your journal: Do you do your best to maintain a high sense of integrity in your work and with colleagues? Do you know when to stop working, before becoming obsessed with work? Do you make each activity in your day a part of your *master plan*? For example, whether you are a school counselor who provides a trusting relationship for children, or a banker who guides people in the right use of prosperity, you have the same opportunity to perform your job with integrity. Even a dishwasher has the opportunity to send a blessing to anyone who eats from his dishes.

2. After being honest with yourself about these questions, notice whether you need to shift your focus. Work can be a wonderful way to express your spirit. Your work does not have to be that of a minister or rabbi to be spiritual. The world needs many different kinds of people to use their talent. See how you are using your abilities today. The thoughts and blessings you put on the work that you do affect every person who comes into contact with it and especially you.

The Master Plan

The *master plan* is the spiritual life plan behind your life purpose. When we act without awareness of the *master plan* for our lives, our egos and personalities tend to be in charge. We get off track because we are driven by our illusions about who we are and what we need instead of being in touch with our true identity. In the following exercise you will begin to identify the *master plan*.

Exercise: Drawing Houses that Reflect Our Master Plan

Goal: Discovering your personal master plan

1. Take out a paper and pencil or, even better, crayons, and draw the house or apartment in which you currently live. Then draw your ideal house and third, draw any house that you can remember having seen recently in a dream. If you have not seen any houses in dreams, skip that step. Do not worry about having artistic ability; just draw the best house that you can at this time. After you complete your drawing of your present house and your desired dream house, recall any dreams you have had during the night about houses or buildings. Write down these dreams about structures, as clearly and in as much detail as you can, recalling as much about the house as possible. You will then gain valuable personal insights in this exercise as you analyze your personal homes and apartments, analyze

your desired or dream houses, and analyze the houses or buildings in your dreams.

Make your drawings as detailed and complete as possible. Let your creativity and imagination flow. Try not to be overanalytical or critical about the process or about your ability to draw.

2. Now, in each case, answer the following questions about your three houses.

 I. Is the house . . .

  a) neat and orderly?

  b) overly neat and clean?

  c) sloppy and disorderly?

  d) chaotic and in complete disarray?

 II. Are the cupboards and drawers . . .

  a) neat and orderly?

  b) overly neat and clean?

  c) sloppy and disorderly?

  d) chaotic and in complete disarray?

 III. Are there significant problems with the . . .

  a) plumbing?

  b) wiring?

  c) structure?

  d) landscape?

 IV. Is the house . . .

  a) overflowing with objects and possessions?

  b) normally full?

  c) sparse and empty?

  d) comfortably sparse?

  e) uncomfortably sparse?

V. What is the condition of the . . .

    a) roof?

    b) floors?

    c) walls?

    d) joists?

    e) bricks?

    f) siding?

    g) porches?

    h) stairs?

VI. Is the house . . .

    a) bright/dark?

    b) dusty/clean?

    c) large/confining?

VII. Describe the condition of the . . .

    a) attic

    b) top floor

    c) main floor

    d) basement

Is each level orderly, well-kept, well-lit or is it the reverse?

Ask yourself these questions about your personal present home, your desired home, and homes you see during the dream state. Then, when you have completed your drawings, take a look to see what they say about your present level of consciousness. Our homes in reality, in dreams, or in desire/imagination are reflections of our perception of self. In this way, we can get in touch with what is going on with us presently in order to get more clear about our blueprint or *master plan*.

The answers to these questions can tell us a great deal about our own present state. The areas where there are similarities among the responses regarding the actual house and dream house are especially important and will help you to assess your present constructive or destructive traits to help you develop the *master plan*.

First, let's address the topic of neatness. In the Asian art of Feng Shui, a cluttered, disorganized house would not be considered conducive to prosperity or harmony. Our environments are reflections of our inner selves and say a great deal about us. If our insides are chaotic, it is reflected in our surroundings. In reverse, a meticulously clean house can represent a particular need to control your surroundings too much. This is also an imbalance in the house. A home which looks lived-in but has a divine order is the most harmonious choice. Correcting neatness issues externally can assist in getting your inner house in order as well. Now examine whether your houses have specific problems. Problems may be with plumbing (overemotional), wiring (burnout), structural (out of sync with the *master plan*), or landscape (manifestation of your thoughts and actions). If the plumbing is leaking, you may not be channeling and directing your emotions. Wires shorting may be related to physical or mental burnout or wiring overload. Nonfunctional electrical outlets represent parts of the house we are not plugged into. Large structural issues suggest we may not be getting the support internally or externally that we need. The yard is a reflection of what we manifest. Is it full and lush or sparse, in need of weeding, or dry? How much we tend to our garden may show how much action we put into manifesting our dreams.

Notice what is in your house. An overly full house may be a sign that you are filling up lonely spaces. It may also be a sign of addiction to possessions. Collections are a fun hobby, so long as the house is not overridden with collections. An empty house may be a healthy sign of detachment from possessions, or a neglect of the self and personal needs. Ask yourself if your needs are being met by a comfortable economy of decor, or if you are simply ignoring your needs.

Floors ground us and give us a foundation; porches are avenues to accessibility; stairs take us from one level of consciousness to another. Are they performing their functions efficiently? Is the house well lit? This is a reflection of welcoming personal illumination. Is it softly lit, reflecting a welcoming softness to yourself? Being in the dark speaks for itself. Perhaps there are things about you that you do not want to recognize or see.

Take a look at the porches in your own drawings. Are you accessible through the porch or are the stairs broke? Do they lead directly to the front door in a highly accessible manner?

Now take a look at the staircases inside the house. Sometimes, in dreams, a staircase leads to nowhere. To which missing floor does the staircase lead? For example, if the stairs lead to the second floor but there is no second floor, it may be a sign that you have not utilized your higher consciousness recently.

Floors are extremely important in the analysis of the house drawings. For example, the first floor represents your living space, or the conscious ego. The second floor represents intellectual understanding, and the attic, your highest level of spiritual understanding, your dreams, and desires. The basement represents the subconscious beliefs. It can also represent the collective unconscious level of mind. In the collective unconscious, there is only one unconscious that is owned by everyone. Because the unconscious is collective, we often tap into other people in our dreams in ways that tell us how they are important to us. As you look at the condition of these floors, you can see which parts of yourself are being expressed.

And then there's the roof and the size of the house. The roof represents our ideas, particularly our intellectual ones. If you have seen a house in a dream state, has someone just stolen the roof off your house, perhaps making you feel that someone has made poor use of your ideas? Then notice the size the house? Are you rattling around in it or do you feel confined? This represents how you are feeling about your life at the present time.

For the houses in your dreams, add the following questions:

1. Where are you in the house during the dream?

2. Is there water near the house?

3. Are parts of the house missing or present, unexplored or open, visible or invisible, dirty or clean, filled or empty?

4. Which floors have people on them?

5. Is there a vehicle near the house?

6. What do you like best about the house?

7. What do you like least about the house?

The purpose of this exercise is to look at the houses and what they reflect about ourselves. For example, a blocked attic in a dream, may represent feelings of inaccessibility to the higher self. A cluttered basement may represent an overloaded subconscious or unconscious. Reviewing what is happening on each of the floors can tell you what each part of the self is currently expressing. Notice where you spend most of your time. For example is it in the higher consciousness (attic)? Is the time you spend there in proportion to the time you spend in the rest of the house or do you spend too much time in dreams and fantasies, in your highest floor?

Is there water near the dream house? This may show how you manage your emotions. Is the water flooding the house? This may suggest you are overwhelmed by feelings. Is there a stagnant pond? You may be weighed down by old unexplored emotions.

If parts of the house are missing or blocked, you may not be aware of the level of consciousness represented by the floor. Is the house full (of awareness and ideas) or empty (void of insight)? Maybe the house is under construction. That means that you are moving through changes which can be positive. Note where people are. If they are in the basement, they may have an influence on you subconsciously. In the attic, they may influence your spiritual life. A dirty or dusty house may mean that the floors of the house that are dusty are unexplored or wounded parts of your consciousness.

A vehicle near the house can be viewed similarly to the house. Does it run well? Is it in good shape? Does it have high horsepower? Or is it broken down or wrecked? The condition of the car reflects your view of the present condition of your life.

Your favorite parts of the dream house show where you feel comfortable with yourself. Is it in the spiritual consciousness (attic), the intellect, (second floor) or with family and friends (first floor)? Is your least favorite part of the house the basement? If so ask yourself what you are avoiding in the subconscious.

The houses in our dream state tell us what is going on in the subconscious and unconscious. Our physical houses represent what we are currently expressing on all levels of consciousness. And our ideal houses represent what we want to express on each and every level of consciousness. The degree to which we are in touch with God's plan for us can be reflected in our awareness of the houses in which we desire to live. Our *master plan* assists us in moving away from disillusionment and pain. Some pain is part of the growth process and part of moving away from disillusionment, but the more we grow, the more we become in touch with the *master plan*. Elizabeth Kübler-Ross, an expert on death and dying, said, "Learn to get in touch with the silence within yourself and know that everything in life has purpose." As we get in touch with our true purpose and move away from the disillusionment which may have occurred as a result of our ego, we move away from the dark night of the soul. This is the period just before the enlightenment begins, in which awareness dawns that we are truly spiritual beings.

Review your assessment of your houses and decide which parts of yourself need growth. You can assist in making the mental and emotional changes by working on your physical house. As you clean the basement, you are constantly reminded to clear your subconscious. As you remove the dust, you are reminded to uncover parts of the self. Each time you see the house with these revisions, you are reminded of the growth process to which you are committed.

In addition, begin to clear up those areas of your consciousness that need work, based on the information you gained in the assessment. Many of the techniques in the trance breaking section of the book will assist you. See the references at the end of the chapter and choose resources that will help you with your goal.

BELIEF IN THE MASTER PLAN

The thing about spiritual truth is that it wants to be spoken. It is too important to be left alone in silence.

—Rabbi Lawrence Kushner,
Opening Wide the Gates of Jewish Mysticism and Spirituality

BELIEVING IN GOD MAY be the greatest gift you can give yourself, or God for that matter. First of all, you will never walk alone again, not from the first time that the *master plan* becomes real for you. Since I began following my *master plan*, I have had many verifications of the existence of my soul, of the presence of my angels, and of the synchronistic events that occur once you accept the plan. An experience from my life that follows may assist you in understanding our spirit and the eternality of the spirit.

I had been vacationing in Chautauqua, New York, following a stressful period at work. I was staying in a rustic cottage on the lake where no telephone was available, so I could not be reached, and that felt like a fine idea at the time. Three days into my vacation, I awakened early, then fell back into a half-asleep state. In this semi-dream-like state, I could see the figure of a ninety-two-year-old man with a handsome face and gray hair, wearing brown slacks and a gold and brown striped shirt. I clearly recognized this man as my grandfather. (My grandfather was alive and quite witty, lively, and full of conversation flavored with his Italian accent. He was an excellent cook, especially when making lasagna or wedding soup.) In the dream, my grandfather entered the room and said to me, "I came to see if you were alright before I left, because you weren't there." He then walked away into a bright light and disappeared. I awakened and made a note of the dream and the date and time of it, and thought about it for a couple of days. When I returned home and talked with my family at the end of the week, I found out that just before the time of my vision, three days after his death, my grandfather's funeral had been held. How wonderful that he had come looking for me to see if I was alright before he left because I was the one he couldn't find at the funeral or elsewhere! It seemed that not only had he visited me while out of body and before making his transition into the afterlife, but he was fully aware, having attended his own funeral, that I was the only one who wasn't there.

This experience fit with a concept I had learned earlier. During my years of intense study of spiritual matters, I had come across the teaching that when someone dies, their spirit does not make a full transition into the afterlife for about three days. This theory is similar to the one in the Christian faith; Jesus died on Good Friday but did not ascend until Easter Sunday. I gained a deeper faith in eternal life of the spirit that day. Once my faith had increased, I was able to live closer to the hub of my *priority wheel*.

After the vision of my grandfather, I remembered a recurring dream I had as a child in which I died, saw my spirit outside of my body, and attended my own funeral. It had not meant much at the time, but now it seemed to make sense. We have a spirit, a spirit that exists with or without our body, a spirit that makes a transition to a higher place where it can continue to grow and transcend. Having this awareness, I contacted my grandmother to review the details of my grandfather's funeral. I learned that the clothing he was wearing in my dream was identical to what he was wearing when he died. As we pursue the spiritual path, our dreams become more and more meaningful. Dreams that we have had many years before may take on new meaning, and the ones we have in the present may reveal important information for our journey.

My conscious awareness of my own spirit came through an interesting experience sometimes referred to an "out-of-body" experience. I had learned that the body and spirit can sometimes be separated momentarily, but if the separation continues too long, we can die. This is similar to "near death experiences," when people see their spirit hovering over their bodies. In these instances, there is often a translucent cord, appearing to be white or silver, between the body and spirit. This cord seems to represent an umbilical cord, which attaches the body to the spirit. Once his cord is severed, the individual generally dies. A friend of mine, who was a Catholic Franciscan Brother, had once described seeing the cord as he sat by the deathbed of a fellow brother. My friend had long been able to see the umbilical cord between the body and spirit and had images of angels and saints walking the grounds at the monastery. As his friend lay dying, he saw the man's spirit leave the body and the cord becoming thinner as the spirit moved further away from the body. Eventually, as his friend died, the cord was broken and the spirit left the room.

In my own experience, I had been napping on a couch in my psychotherapy office one afternoon when a patient of one of my colleagues suddenly burst into the waiting room. She had a serious psychological disorder known as schizophrenia with paranoid delusions. She often heard voices telling her that someone was trying to hurt her. When she could not find her therapist, she assumed that someone had taken her and was trying to hurt her. She pounded on my office door loudly and began screaming at me, demanding to know what I had done with her therapist, who she assumed I had hidden from her. I awoke with a start and felt myself fly off the couch onto the floor, where I sat looking up at her. I could not move or speak clearly, but I kept repeating her name, unable to get anything else out. At that point, I realized that I was looking at myself on the floor from the couch as clearly as if I had been looking in a mirror. My spirit was still on the couch looking at my body on the floor. I had been thrown out of my body! After several seconds, when my spirit worked its way back into my body, I was able to speak, move, and then handle the situation.

These experiences reinforced my faith that the spirit exists separate from the body. This again assured me of the eternality of the spirit. As you move forward on the path, many things will help you to know that the spirit is eternal. My own experiences will assist your faith as you move on to discover your own *master plan*.

Encouragement Notes

- If you have been writing in your journal, congratulate yourself. It is the first step in self-awareness.

- Experience the sense of joy your prayer statement brings you. You can add to it when you have new positive experiences, insights, spiritual group meetings, etc.

- Notice the benefit of making your prayer statement daily.

- Check out something from the reference list at the end of the chapter that captivates you and enjoy it.

- Tune into the evidence of God in your life this week. What did you experience, feel, sense, touch that got you in touch with your spirit? What did you sense intuitively? Thank the Divine for evidence of His/Her presence. Enjoy the sense of gratefulness and fullness this evidence brings to you. It can come from anything in your life: nature, other people, a quiet meditation, etc.

RESOURCES FOR CHAPTER ONE

Books

The Artist's Way at Work. Julia Cameron, Mark Bryan and
   Catherine Allen, William Morrow and Company: NY,
   1998.

*The Gift of Prayer: A Treasury of Personal Prayer from the
   World's Spiritual Traditions.* Continuum: NY, 1995.

Ageless Body, Timeless Mind. Deepak Chopra, Harmony
   Books: NY, 1993.

Why Zebras Don't Get Ulcers. Robert M. Sapolsky, Freeman:
   NY, 1994.

Waking Up in Time. Peter Russell, Origin Press: Novato, CA,
   1992.

The Cloister Walk. Kathleen Norris, Riverhead Books: NY,
   1996.

Are You the One for Me? Barbara DeAngelis, Dell: NY, 1992.

The Accidental Buddhist. Dinty W. Moore, Doubleday: NY,
   1997.

Siddhartha. Herman Hesse, Bantam: NY, 1951.

Coyote Medicine. Lewis Mehl-Madrona M.D., Scribner: NY,
   1997.

Eight Weeks to Optimum Health. Andrew Weil, Alfred Knopf:
   NY, 1997.

Interior Castles. St. Theresa of Avila, Translated by Allison
   Peersf, Image Books: NY, 1989.

The Immune Power Personality. Henry Dreher, Plume: NY,
   1996.

The Pleasure Connection: How Endorphins Affect Our Health and Happiness. Deva and James Beck, R.N., Synthesis, San Marco, CA, 1987.

Spontaneous Healing. Andrew Weil, Alfred Knopf: NY, 1995.

Creating Money: Keys to Abundance. H. J. Kramer, Tiburon, CA, 1988.

Creation of Health. C. Norman Shealy and Caroline M. Myss, M.A., Stillpoint: Walpole, NH, 1988.

Heal Your Body. Louise L. Hay, Hay House: Santa Monica, 1982.

Organizations

Institute of Noetic Sciences, Sausalito, CA

Music

Chariots of Fire, Vangelis

On Wings of Song, Robert Gass

Fanfare for the Common Man, Aaron Copeland

Gregorian Chant, Franciscan Monks

Gandhi soundtrack

2

Please Don't Quote Me

I am never upset for the reason I
think I am.

—Gerald Jampolsky

Riches You Will Gain from This Chapter

- Awareness of old negative "trances" that hypnotized you into unhappiness

- Knowledge of how to change old trances

- Understanding of how you personally see the world through your senses

- Making a deep commitment to your spiritual self

PERCEPTUAL FILTERS

HOW YOU HEAR WHAT I am saying is the result of many years of the forming of your personal perceptions. Everything you read is seen, heard, and felt through the filter of that perception. Like static on the television screen, you see only the part of the picture that your perceptual filter allows you to see. The static also alters what you see and changes its form. That is how most of life is lived. If you don't believe it, look at your words and see if they don't match the outcomes in your life. Say, "I'm never going to find a new job," and believe it with all of your energy, and you may just have that exact experience.

Our interpretation of others' behavior is based on our personal insecurities and preconceived notions. We rarely consider that others' actions are in no way based on our insecurities, but on their own energy.

Why is it so hard at times to get back to our spirit? How do we get off our path in the first place? A famous hypnotist, Milton H. Erickson, formed the foundation for much of the current practice of hypnosis. He said, "Life is consecutive hypnosis." He meant that our minds are given perceptions that we accept as realities and that we live our lives from these perceptions for better or for worse. When we were treated well, as children, we were given positive messages which we incorporated into our consciousness as positive realities. We then live with positive expectations about our lives. Conversely, if we were given messages that were destructive to our self-image, we accepted those also and began to expect mistreatment. None of these beliefs, positive or negative, are necessarily true or false. But once we fall into the trance of believing them, we act from that moment as if they are true. Erickson studied these false beliefs, which he referred to as "hypnotic trances," and became a master at breaking false or destructive trances.

Erickson's followers, Richard Bandler and John Grinder, wrote several books about his trance-breaking techniques. One of those books, *Frogs into Princes*, describes the necessity to break those hypnotic trances. A frog has very narrow slits for eyes and little peripheral vision. Since a frog exists mainly on flies, it is necessary to have a constant supply of these insects. But because a frog has such narrow vision, it may be completely surrounded by flies, with some on top of its head, and yet it can literally starve to death if the flies don't fly in front of the frog's face. We are much like the frog. We are starving to death even more seriously, because the particular flies we think we need in order to exist are not visible in our narrow perception. You do not have to remain that way! As a matter of fact,

we will use Ericksonian techniques to break these
trances now.

Exercise: Trance Identification

Goal: To identify old trances that are ineffective

1. Answer the following questions in your journal.
   What was it you were told you had to do or be
   as a child in order to be valuable or acceptable
   to others? What particular "hypnotic trance"
   are you in which prevents you from seeing your
   worth and the good in your life? If you were
   taught that you had to have a certain amount
   of money to have value, many other opportuni-
   ties for things, such as love, personal growth,
   peace of mind, or good health may fly unseen
   into your narrow vision, and you will starve to
   death because you lack self-approval and acceptance. You may be rejecting other forms of fulfillment because they don't fit your original
   trance that said that money was the most necessary commodity for your life.

2. Check off from the following list any negative
   trances that may fit your present thinking.

   ____ I will not be successful or happy because I
   am . . . (underline as many as apply) a man,
   a woman, a member of a minority, poor,
   lacking in background or education, not
   smart enough, not popular enough, not
   good looking enough, addicted, unstable,
   too old, too young, not good enough, other.

___ Other people's needs are more important
than my own.

___ I will not be able to support myself doing
what I love.

___ I will fail because I failed before.

___ No one will ever love me.

___ If I do what I want, my partner
(or mother, father, kids, friends, colleagues)
will disapprove.

___ Other: Add your own.

Step one on the journey is to ask yourself, What is
my trance? Is it healthy for me? Is it constructive? Is it
what I would have truly chosen for myself if I could
choose any trance at all? Do I need any trance at all?
After you have written the answers to these questions,
accept that it is possible to let them go.

Many self-help books are designed to help us get
what we want. There is a useful and valuable purpose
here, but what if what we want is a destructive trance?
What if our true self and our trance about who we are
supposed to be and what we are supposed to have do
not match? Shall we live in depression because we are
not obtaining what we want, or should we change our
belief?

In other cases, our identity is so tied up in what we
want that our existence in our own minds is dependent
upon having it. You might spend a life feeling insecure
because the thing you most need might escape or elude

you. Placing your happiness on having whatever your trance is may cause constant insecurities. If losing the desired person, job, or outcome would cause a loss of the self as it exists in our minds, we may be having a destructive trance. This is the cause of much sadness and depression.

A lovely woman I knew named Katie had been given a trance when her parents convinced her that she must marry a wealthy man, take her position in society, and let him take care of her. She was a very sensitive, talented, spiritual person, a cellist, and an ideal friend with an eye for art and beauty. She was the envy of those who had the opportunity to know her. And when the trance she was given eluded her, she became despondent, then depressed, then suicidal, and finally physically ill, all the while mourning the loss of her dream. She was never able to step aside, view herself objectively, see the trance, recognize it as such, and break free of it.

Do you remember your first dreams of what you wanted to be when you grew up? The very first one before anyone influenced you? What stemmed from your own conscious mind about who you were and wanted to be? Can you gain information from this that would assist you with knowing your true self? Then ask yourself, if you could do or be whatever you want right now, free of limitations, what would you be?

Exercise: Viewing Your Trance

Goal: To objectively view your current trance.

1. Try this exercise to help you discover and break your trance. Close your eyes and take a couple of deep breaths. Visualize a screen on your mind. It can be a TV screen, a movie screen, a computer screen, whatever you prefer. On this screen play a movie of your life at present, and view the movie as if you were an objective third party, watching and observing someone else's life. What do you notice? What drives and motivates you? What is it that you must have or be? How is that helping or hurting you? In general, what trances are you living out? Let it be conscious. Is it a dream of your parents? Your spouse? Some mixture of those awarenesses? What is going on, on the screen? How is it affecting you positively? Negatively?

2. Ask yourself, what would you like to do differently? It is not essential to know exactly how to make things different or what to make different at this point; it is just necessary to see what the trance is, to hear what the directives are, to feel what is happening. There is a part of your mind that knows what to change and how to change it, and we will activate that part of your mind later. For now, let us learn a bit about our minds. Let us write the owner's manual that we wish would have come with our minds at birth.

REPRESENTATIONAL SYSTEMS:
HOW WE FORM TRANCES

Nothing has meaning except that which you assign
to it.

—Cheatwood Research Institute

TO MORE CLEARLY UNDERSTAND our trances, both constructive and destructive ones, we need to know the
three major ways in which we store our trances. There
are three basic representational systems by which we
can interpret incoming or internal data. These are auditory (hearing), visual (seeing), and kinesthetic (feeling).
Information is primarily channeled through these three
systems. Taste and smell are also systems for information, but our auditory, visual, and kinesthetic are the
primary ones. Most of us have a preference for one of
these systems and use one or two systems more than
the third. The ideal situation is to have full use of all
three faculties, giving you many resources through
which you can channel information. It is like having a
three-legged stool. When all three legs are the same
length, the stool is most balanced and supports us best.

I know a musician whose three systems are wide
open. She hears whole original symphonies in her
mind, visualizes all of the parts for the different instru-
ments scored on paper, and kinesthetically feels how
the pieces ought to be played. Obviously, this makes
her quite a talented and resourceful individual. We,
too, can become truly resourceful in creating our lives,

even in running our minds, by learning to use all of our systems. First, let's take a look at where we are now to find out, once again, where we are going. This helps us to move our frogs along into princes or princesses!

To increase our awareness of our representational systems and how we use them, remember that you probably have one system that is your main or primary system, another which is your secondary system, and a third which is your least used system. In the descriptions that follow, identify which traits suit you most, which are second most like you, and which are tertiary or least used.

Visual people (visuals) have to see everything, and often they hold their heads up and stand very straight in order to see things. Visuals have much better recall for conversations held in person instead of on the phone because they saw the person to whom they were speaking. They speak quickly because they get pictures of all they want to say and have to get it all out before they lose their picture. They learn by seeing. They move quickly, come and go quickly, and are distracted by movement. They use visual words when speaking (see what I mean, watch this, point of view, that's a cloudy, fuzzy, clear, or bright idea). Visuals may not have any difficulty working around background noise, but if somebody walks across the room, their attention is completely diverted. They use common phrases to describe visual situations, such as, "I get the picture," "Focus on this," "Showing off," "That's clear to me." Their world is represented in a picturesque fashion and their words show it. If a highly visual person cannot see you when you talk, they may miss much of what you say.

If you have decided that this is most like you, then you are "getting the picture." If it is least like you, then some other things may be going on. You may have been led in a more auditory or kinesthetic style by early life experiences and found those modalities to be more acceptable to you, or you may have shut down visually due to witnessing visually unpleasant occurrences. These possibilities apply to all least used systems whether they are auditory, visual, or kinesthetic.

Someone with a primarily auditory experience of the world wants to hear everything. Auditories pick up conversations of people nearby, they hear music in the background, and when in conversation, tilt their head toward you in order to tune in better. They speak in a monotone but surround themselves with people who have interesting, varied sounding voices. Because we can only listen to one thing at a time (in contrast to visuals who can see many pictures at a time), auditories may not be listening to you if they are talking to themselves. They may even tilt their head sideways and then lean on their hand in an "on the phone" type of image. They use self-help tapes more than books when in a growth period. They do one thing at a time and finish it before moving on. They are more organized, sequential, and logical than other types. They often have arithmetic ability. They use auditory words and experiences when speaking: "ring, sputter, resonate, or buzz" and "hear what you are saying," "it rings true," and "sounds good to me."

Now, let's move onto kinesthetic people. If an object or concept is not meaningful to kinesthetics, then it really isn't important. Physical possessions are only important if there is a sentimental attachment. Facts and figures are only relevant is they have meaning. For example, a kinesthetic does not care when the beginning of the manufacturing industry occurred, but would never forget their wedding anniversary. They speak with emotion, touch things, gesture, touch you when speaking, play with their hair, and are relationship-oriented. They often speak rather disjointedly in phrases. They talk about physical sensations or feeling things: "hard cold facts," "getting a handle on things," "good vibrations," "concrete data," their "hands may be tied," or they may want to "get a grip." They make decisions based on whether or not things "feel" right.

Now, if you have not decided which is most like you, consider the following information. When we are thinking in an auditory, kinesthetic, or visual fashion, our eyes move to different positions. When thinking visually, they move up; auditorally, out to the ears; and when being kinesthetic, our eyes look down.

Even when you are conscious of these movement tendencies, they still occur. Try a simple exercise to see if you notice your eyes moving to different positions.

1. Imagine your mother wearing a purple hat up in a tree cooking dinner.

2. Recall the words of your favorite song.

3. Remember how you felt the day you moved out of your childhood family home.

4. Imagine the look of your kitchen in detail.

5. How does your voice sound under water?

6. How would you feel if your dreams came true?

Did you notice that your eyes moved to different positions to access different information? What if you looked up to the visual position when thinking about your favorite song? You chose to visualize something that is usually auditory, so perhaps you are a visual. Did you look down to the kinesthetic position when you were trying to picture something? Perhaps the important thing in your recollection was your feeling about the picture. Could you be primarily kinesthetic?

Exercise: Identifying Your Representational System

Goal: Using past memory to determine in which representational system they are stored.

With a partner, try the following exercise. Let your partner watch your eye position and listen to your words. Have your partner write down what they hear and observe as you speak. See if they can add additional information to help you decide what your primary, secondary, and tertiary, or least used, systems are. You can write your answers down yourself if there is no one who can help you with this exercise at this time. First tell your partner about a place you have been that you might say is your favorite place. For the second part of the exercise tell your partner about the first car (or book or house) you ever owned that was yours alone.

Sample Dialogues

Dialogue 1

Direction: Tell me about a favorite place that you have been.

Response: The Bahamas . . . clear water . . . sunny skies . . . really warm . . . beautiful walks and sand in your toes.

This description is primarily kinesthetic and, while some pictures are taken into consideration, the phrasing and short disjointed nature of the conversation suggests a primary kinesthetic style with a secondary visual style.

Dialogue 2

Direction: Tell me about your first car.

Response: My first car was a 1969 Mustang with a four-cylinder engine and it had 27,000 miles on it when we bought it. It was purchased on June 14 of that year and it only broke down twice before I sold it five years later to a man from Memphis, Tennessee.

This dialogue is reflective of an extremely auditory style. It has many details, including all of the proper numbers, and is extremely specific and logical in its description. We did not learn about the appearance of the car, nor how the person felt about their automobile.

Dialogue 3

Direction: Describe a favorite vacation spot.

Response: You should have seen it there. There were plants of a tropical nature everywhere. They were extremely colorful in bright fuchsias and blues and oranges. Then there was the snorkeling trip. The fish were so many colors and the water was so warm you felt like you were in an aquarium with them.

This is primarily a visual person with a secondary kinesthetic view of life. They present many pictures, and you can actually see in your mind the things they are describing. And they also tell you how they feel about things, both physically (warm water) and emotionally.

CHANGING TRANCES

By acknowledging previously rejected parts of ourselves, we assume greater responsibility for our lives.

—Ronald S. Miller, *As Above So Below*

WHAT DO WE DO with all of this information and why is it important? This information may hold the keys to your personal and spiritual growth. For one thing, all of our negative self-images, hurts, traumas, and stresses are recalled in an auditory, visual, and kinesthetic fashion. They are dependent upon past memories that may or may not be conscious. When we recall them we can change them. The same is true for our positive self-images and concepts. They only exist as we have stored them. If we can soften or take power away from the negative memories, then we can heal ourselves and move on. The next time you become upset, notice what you are thinking. Are you picturing something, telling yourself something, or having a feeling about the picture or verbal message? In what system is the pain or discomfort? What do you need to do to change what you are seeing, hearing, or feeling? Notice how you walk, stand, hold your body, breathe, and talk, when you are upset.

Choose an old traumatic event to release today, not something too stressful, but something that is mildly upsetting. Once you have picked a memory, be sure it is only mildly stressful. If traumas stem from the memories, do not do the exercise by yourself. It can be too frightening or harmful. The purpose of the exercise is for healing, and if the memory makes you too frightened, you may not be able to work through it. Be sure you feel safe healing these traumas before you begin the exercises. If something is so stressful or upsetting that even thinking about it makes you anxious, panicky, or self-destructive, do not do the following exercise on your own. Let a trained professional help you.

You may feel that healing is taking place even now with this particular trauma. You can recall an unpleasant or negative incident that is safe to remember and go through a healing process with visualization. Since the mind stores only what we put in it, it is likely to react in the future as though our imagined ending is real. The mind does not differentiate what has happened from what is imagined. This is a good way to change things we regret or that haunt us into things that are put to rest. This is essential for our mental, emotional, and physical health.

When you are feeling imbalances such as anger, fear, hopelessness, loneliness, defeat, security, etc., you can use this visualization to help heal anything that may be a block or interference to your growth. You may even see ways that this pattern has taught you important lessons, which in some way may have assisted you in your growth. As you release hurts of the past, if you have benefited in some way from the situation, you may become aware of it. Early in life, much too early, I married, and the marriage ended, but I redirected my energy into my work, something I might not have done if I had not had to end the marriage. A highly effective recipe for turning adversity into a gift is to heal the old pain, give thanks for the lesson learned, forgive everyone involved, and move forward. This cycle of healing, releasing, understanding, giving thanks, and forgiving allows movement and a complete healing of a negative pattern. Mental

practice and visualization can create a new way of per-
ceiving your life.

Practicing mentally often results in an improved
performance in our lives. It changes the way we store
information. In Timothy Galway's books *Inner Tennis,
Inner Skiing,* and *Inner Golf,* we can rehearse our performance in athletic situations or even business situations and actually allow our mind to experience a
"practice effect." The same is true in personal situations. If we rehearse the way we want to behave in a
particular situation, we are more likely to believe that
we have done so in the past and can do so again. If a
particular situation has had a negative outcome, we
can visualize and imagine it with a positive outcome,
allowing our mind to accept that things did not have
to be as bad as, in fact, they were. The following three
exercises are useful for a single unpleasant incident or
a recurring pattern that we would like to change. Be
sure the trauma is not too upsetting so you can complete the exercise on your own.

Exercise One: Identify and Change an Old Belief

Goal: To determine which representational system
carries an old memory.

1. Imagine the last time that someone hurt your
   feelings. Remember what was said, playing the
   scene in your mind, and feeling the feelings you
   had then.

2. Now, imagine what you need to do to change this memory. What do you need to say to this person? To yourself? What do you need to see happening? How do you need to picture the change in order to see a positive outcome?

3. Now notice how you feel about the outcome you are imagining. Accept this new positive ending, and visualize the new scene with the new dialogue and feeling levels. Allow it to sink into your thinking as truth. Then notice how you feel tomorrow after you have lived with this new positive outcome for a day . . . then a week . . . a month . . . and a year. Allow yourself to recreate the situation, seeing yourself handling the situation exactly as you want to, feeling the feelings that you want to feel, and hearing the words that you need to hear.

Exercise Two: Starting Over

Goal: Breaking an old trance and making a new one.

1. Think of a time when you felt completely relaxed. You will want to fully associate and recall all of your feelings of relaxation in order to attach yourself to those feelings. Then recall everything you could see at that time of relaxation, then everything you could hear. By this time, you should be fully associated with that time of relaxation and may be feeling completely relaxed.

2. Now recall one specific time when you were having fun. Remember how it felt to have fun, and
fully associate with and recall that feeling. Then
recall all the sounds you heard as you were having fun, even sounds you may not have paid
attention to at the time. Then recall all you
could see as you were having fun, all the colors
and shapes. Enjoy being there . . . having fun
now.

3. Move on to a specific time when you were doing
something and knew you were doing it well and
were feeling successful. It can be anything at all
and doesn't have to be a huge accomplishment.
It can be getting bills paid on time, succeeding
with a new recipe, or remembering how to tie
your shoe. What is important is, big or small,
the event made you feel successful. Recall those
feelings of success now. Remember what you
could see as you were being successful, and
then remember what you could hear, especially
things you may have been telling yourself about
being relaxed, having fun, and being successful.

4. Now allow yourself to recall a pattern you
would like to change, perhaps a tendency to
trust people too quickly or a habit of feeling
anxious at certain times, anything that is a pattern that you would like to change. Then think
of a time recently when you exhibited this pattern. See and hear it in your mind. As you
observe, imagine that you are watching the
whole situation on a screen of any type: movie,
television, computer, etc. As you observe, see

what you might want to change. You are the
producer, director, and script writer. Imagine
how you would like to recreate the scene. Then
watch the new outcome. See it, feel it, hear it,
believe it, know it, and catch on enthusiastically
with the acceptance of it on every level.

   If you are having difficulty, note which parts
of you may disbelieve that you deserve a positive
outcome or what part of you may not feel safe
being successful. Talk to that part of yourself.
What kind of reassurance does that part of you
need in order to feel better? Can you give that
part of you reassurance? If not, is there anyone
you know who can? Imagine that person giving
the fearful or insecure part of you the assurance
that you need in order to make changes now.

5. When you feel fully satisfied that you have han-
   dled the situation in any way which is positive,
   let your mind move back in time to a moment
   before this recent incident when you felt the
   same pattern getting in your way. Go through
   the same procedure for handling the situation.
   When you are fully satisfied that you have created a new image of the situation in a positive
   fashion, then go back to another incident in
   time before that one when the same problem
   got in your way, and complete the process again.
   Continue going backward until you get to the
   bottom of the pattern, perhaps the first time
   that it occurred, and continue to heal the pattern in the same way. Then notice how you feel
   having used your creativity, resourcefulness, and

talent to solve this problem. Notice that your
solution has integrated itself into your mind
and become a part of you. See, hear, and feel
yourself stand, walk, talk, move, and breathe the
way you will when you have fully integrated this
change into yourself. Notice that by tomorrow,
it feels and is even more a part of you. Notice
how that change manifests in your feelings and
in your life by next week . . . next month . . . six
months from now . . . next year. And now return
to the present.

Exercise Three: Clearing the Screen

Goal: Identifying the ways in which healing
could empower you.

Ask yourself the following questions and wait for
the answers to arise. Be sure you are in a very relaxed
setting and are not going to be interrupted.

1. What would you do if you could do anything at
   all, if there were no limitations?

2. If your purpose in life was to be happy, what
   would you do?

3. What was the first thing you ever wanted to do
   or be in your life? Think back before outside
   influences had affected you. Let your mind drift
   back through your various career interests in
   life to find the first thing that ever felt right,
   your first awareness of a way in which you
   wanted to express yourself, when we shall say

"the force" was with you, before events may have
caused you to forget or trances redirected you.

These are questions which will quite likely lead you
to your spiritual purpose, to the *master plan* which will
direct your mind, emotions, and body toward wellness. Healing old inner pain will allow you to get more
in touch with these desires, and they are truly a part of
the *master plan*!

You may feel a lot of fear, of being who you truly are,
the fear of others' reactions, or fear of failure. These
fears are our programming to fail. Barbara Sher, author
of *Live the Life You Love*, even assures you that when you
move forward into a dream, you will surely encounter
resistance from others. Those others are afraid of losing
you and are afraid you may become an example of what
they might have been had they followed their dreams. If
you know their resistance is coming, you are better able
to prepare for it. Sher recommends finding a group of
supportive people to meet with on a regular basis who
will offer the kind of loving support that is needed to
manifest your dreams, which are a reflection of the *master plan*.

If you are having Spiritual Fitness group meetings
or have a Spiritual Fitness partner, you can enhance
your growth. Meeting with people of like mind is one
of the suggestions in the section on "How to Use this
Book." It is an excellent way to break old ineffective
trances. You are investing time in talking about and
affirming your new consciously chosen trances with

people who are doing the same. You are using your life in a way that affirms your spiritual commitment. This is important to do once you set your goal to have new constructive beliefs.

Other spiritual groups with similar purposes are already in existence. The Unity Church sponsors a "Master Mind" group that is based on the teachings of *A Course in Miracles*. The Master Mind group is based on programs for breaking addictions and setting up new behavior patterns. Addictions are defined as anything that we are involved in that keeps us from manifesting our dreams. Each member of the group holds your goal in their mind and sees it as a reality. They dream for you the dreams you hold for yourself. In the course, you have an opportunity to study ways to break addictive programming and live from love without fear.

Personally, I have initiated local community groups for the Institute of Noetic Sciences (IONS). IONS was founded by astronaut Edgar Mitchell and others for the purpose of knowing (the word noetic comes from "knowing") the spiritual connections to the earth and the study of spiritual consciousness. It assists with research of the understanding of changing perceptions about health, science, and spirituality. Once you get a group of people together who are of like mind, and who want their lives to be driven by an ever increasing awareness of their *master plan*, the mutual beliefs of the members form a group consciousness which supports the whole purpose of the group. This accelerates the spiritual, mental, and personal growth of each member. Study groups such as IONS or Master Mind offer the support and growth you need and may not be able to find individually or in your pre-existing groups because of the resistance of others close to you. Remember, when your growth causes those around you to grow in ways in which they need to grow, all are benefited. For example, going to an IONS study group may allow your significant other to spend private time with the children, or work on their own personal goals. Find out if there is an IONS study group in your area, or join IONS and start one.

Another part of your spiritual commitment to Spiritual Fitness is your *daily practice*. The practice already includes your original prayer statement that you set up in chapter 1. The next exercise will add affirmations to your *daily practice*.

Exercise: Expanding Daily Practice

Goal: Adding trance breaking affirmations to the daily practice.

Write in your journal a goal for Spiritual Fitness that reflects a new trance you are adopting. Write it in a positive manner. For example, state your belief as "I am strong and capable" instead of stating that you are not weak or helpless. Write as many of these new trance statements as you like. They will be the second step in your *daily practice*. As you read each one of the affirmations, visualize how it will

feel when it is completely true. Feel that it is completely true now. Feel the feelings you would feel
when it is totally true as if it already is. Hear what
you will hear when it is completely true. What will
you be saying to yourself? Do this affirmation exercise after you have read and re-experienced your
prayer statement.

COMMITMENT

Whatever you can do, or dream you can, begin it.
Boldness has genius, power, and magic in it.

—Goethe

ONCE YOU VERBALIZE THAT you are accepting the *master
plan* for your life, you will not have to walk the path to
Spiritual Fitness alone. Stating your intention and
your purpose puts you in touch with your spiritual
energy and connects that spiritual energy with the
energy in the universe. Staying close to your intention
for life allows you to experience the awareness of your
own intuition. Your intuition, which is a manifestation of your spirit, will help you in ways you never
thought possible.

Commit now to live your life from your higher self,
not from your personality or ego. Say it out loud.
Write it in your journal. Say it to a supportive, loving
group of people. Step out on the path. Assist yourself
by surrounding yourself with high level sensory input.
Visually place pictures and symbols around you that

keep you in touch with your spirit. These may be personal symbols, such as pictures or objects from your religious practice, or even more universal symbols such as angels. Keep nature in your field of vision such as plants, flowers, and animals.

This poem from the Scottish Himalayan Expedition may be an excellent point to focus on in order to help direct yourself each and every day toward your commitment to your *master plan.*

> *Until one is committed, there is hesitancy,*
> *the chance to draw back*
> *Always ineffectiveness concerning*
> *all acts of initiative (and creation)*
> *There is one elementary truth*
> *The ignorance of which kills countless ideas*
> *and splendid plans;*
> *The moment one definitely commits oneself,*
> *Then providence moves too.*
> *All sorts of things occur to help one*
> *That would never otherwise have occurred.*
> *A whole stream of events issues from the decision*
> *Raising in one's favor all manner of unforeseen*
> *incidents and meetings*
> *And material assistance, which no man*
> *could have dreamt*
> *Would come his way.*

> —Scottish Himalayan Expedition
> W. H. Murray, J. M. Dent & Sons, Ltd., 1951

Encouragement Notes

- What trances have you identified that you are choosing not to keep? What affirmations have you set up to break the old trances and set up new ones? Feel how good it feels to state your new affirmations. Let your mind notice how many positive things can occur with the new trance. See it clearly, hear it, and feel it now. Let yourself be happy about it.

- Act today as if your new trance were true, already. Walk, sit, breathe, smile, speak, and dress as you would if the new affirmation was already a complete part of you.

- Have fun noticing all the things you can notice now that you have a new trance. Feel grateful for it, enjoy it, play with it, and be creative about it.

- Sit back and enjoy the new trance.

RESOURCES FOR CHAPTER TWO

Books

Unlimited Power. Anthony Robbins, Fireside: NY, 1997.

Emotional Alchemy: How the Mind Can Heal the Heart. Tara Bennett-Goleman, Three Rivers Press: NY, 2001.

Frogs into Princes: Neurolinguistic Programming. Richard Bandler and John Grinder, Real People Press: Moab, Utah, 1979.

Kiss Sleeping Beauty Goodbye. Madonna Kolbenschlag, Bantam: NY, 1981.

Using Your Brain for a Change. Richard Bandler, Real People Press: Moab, Utah, 1985.

Reframing: Neurolinguistic Programming and the Transformation of Meaning. Richard Bandler and John Grinder, Real People Press: Moab, Utah, 1981.

Change Your Mind and Keep the Change. Steve and Connie Andreas, Real People Press: Moab, Utah, 1987.

The Aladdin Factor. Jack Canfield and Mark Victor Hansen, Berkley, NY, 1995.

Trance-Formations. Richard Bandler and John Grinder, Real People Press: Moab, Utah, 1981.

Music

Yo-Yo Ma, *The Cello Suites Inspired by Bach*

Johann Pachelbel, *Canon in D*

Antonio Vivaldi, *Flute Concertos*

Halo, *Visions of Angels*

George F. Handel, *The Messiah*

Samuel Barber, *Classical Occasions*

Maurice Ravel, *The Fairy Garden*

3

The Ways of
Spiritual Fitness

Breath is Life.

—Yogi Ramacharaka

Riches You Will Gain from This Chapter

- Learning to breathe to heal your mind and body and to feel your spirit

- Knowledge of how to use color, music, sound, and movement to reach Spiritual Fitness

BREATHING

WE ARE COMPLETELY DEPENDENT upon breathing for our continued existence. No matter which method of relaxation or rejuvenation you study, breathing will be the foundation. It is the fastest, most effective, and least expensive way to activate your awareness of the mind body connection.

Over time, we "forget" how to breathe. We continue to breathe involuntarily, but forget how to breathe naturally, deeply, and diaphragmatically, the way a newborn infant does. Tension, stress, worry, negative thoughts, and lack of rest all create imbalances in our breathing that become chronic patterns. You've heard, "I was so scared I held my breath." Or, "I waited with bated breath." "That was a breath of fresh air." Our thoughts and physical reactions to stress really do recreate our breathing patterns. By the time we reach adulthood, these patterns become fixed, depriving us of breath, "Chi," or the energy of our life force. It is interesting to watch people's faulty breathing patterns. They contain jerks, hesitations, pauses, unevenness, and shallowness. These are all reactions to the chronic stress of life.

How do we begin to escape the chronic stress of life to correct the problem? Twenty to thirty minutes a day of mental and physical inactivity. That means you have no action and no thoughts except for thinking about your breath. You do not make to-do lists, get upset with coworkers, remember things you forgot, or plan strategies. These thoughts may arrive, but you just let them pass and refocus on your breath. Thoughts arouse the sympathetic nervous system that tells the body there is a demand in the environment we must meet. This causes adrenaline to flow, increases heart rate, shortens breath, and may cause sweating, a short temper, and many other symptoms.

Exercise: Symptom Checklist

Goal: To identify your first symptom of a stress response.

Check the following list to see which symptoms you exhibit first when you are under stress.

The keyword is, first, not when you have a stomachache, headache, or back pain, but when you first have a stressful thought or experience. By the time you are in pain, you have been under stress for several minutes, hours, days, or years. If the pain is chronic, then so is the stress.

Rapid heartbeat	*Sweaty hands*
Clenching teeth	*Talking rapidly*
Sudden silences	*Rapid, shallow breathing*

Fidgeting	*Playing with small objects*
Dry mouth	Can't think/Concentrate
Stuttering	*Red skin blotches*
Quick to anger	Sleeplessness
Pain/Headaches/ Stomachaches	Muscle tightness
Physically exhausted	Emotionally exhausted
Wiped out	Unhappy
Depressed	Irritable
Hopeless	Withdrawn
Aggressive verbally	*Aggressive physically*
Constant complaining	Giving up
Rationalizing about your life	Immature behavior
Drinking, smoking	Abusing prescription medicine

The symptoms in italics are the first ones. Have you identified your first symptom? Good. Now you are in a place to know when to begin changing your breath, to interrupt the stress response that you are experiencing. If the symptom is not in italics, then it is a sign of more advanced stress.

As soon as the stress symptom occurs, whatever and whenever it occurs, is the time to intervene by deeply breathing. Your body will respond immediately, especially if you have been doing twenty to thirty minutes of daily breathing practice. Breath training is like training for a race. You would not just run a

marathon without a lot of training ahead of time.
The same is true of breath. Once you have retrained
your body to breathe deeply and evenly, it will do so
when you direct it to. This brings into action your
parasympathetic nervous system, which is the part
of your body that requires twenty minutes to heal,
restore, and rejuvenate your body. A twenty- to
thirty-minute practice removes stress from your
body long enough to allow all the systems of the
body to rest and heal. It is wonderful for healing any
health condition.

Exercise: Diaphragmatic Breathing

Goal: To restore relaxation and health through
deep breathing.

1. Begin by making sure that you are breathing
   through the nose and not the mouth. Nose
   breathing activates the parasympathetic
   nervous system, or the part of the body that
   relaxes. Breathing through the mouth activates
   shallow breathing and a stress response in the
   body. Then begin by paying attention to your
   breath . . . as soon as you direct your attention
   to your breath, it begins to change and slow.
   Observe as it comes and goes. Count the number of seconds it takes to inhale and the number it takes to exhale now. Regulate the breath
   so that the length of the inhale and the length
   of the exhale are the same. Breathe in through
   the nose with the mouth closed. Bring the

breath down into the diaphragm (below, not
into the lungs or chest) and exhale. Increase
the length of the inhale and exhale each by
one count, slowing and deepening the breath.

2. If it is difficult to bring the breath into the
diaphragm, try lying on your stomach with
your chin propped up on your elbows. In this
position, the body naturally breathes diaphragmatically. This will give you the sense and
rhythm of the diaphragmatic breath. Then you
can sit or lie in order to continue your breathing
practice, continuing to breathe deeply into the
diaphragm. Do this several times. Is it comfortable to breathe at a slower, deeper rate? Do not
try to force yourself to breathe more deeply than
is comfortable. Then, if you are comfortable,
increase the length of the inhale and the length
of the exhale each by one more count. Breathe in
this way a few more times, if it feels comfortable.
If thoughts come into your mind, release them as
you exhale. You will notice that fewer thoughts
will enter your mind once you have slowed the
breath. Continue this slow, deep breathing
actively for twenty or thirty minutes until you
feel calm, restored, and relaxed.

It is important to bring the breath into the
diaphragm first. If the diaphragm is full and
you continue breathing, you can fill the chest
with air secondly. This activates the body's
relaxation response. As you are lying down,
place one hand on the diaphragm and one
hand on the chest to feel whether you are

breathing fully. One way to jump start the body
into diaphragmatic breathing is to lie in the
position that was indicated earlier with your
chin propped up on your elbows. In this position, you will automatically breathe diaphragmatically. You can feel the diaphragm expand
and fill.

Breathing can be a holy and transformative practice. No matter what relaxation technique you use, it
centers around the breath. It is the central and most
important spiritual practice you can do, and it's free!
The breath is evidence of the spirit. Once the breath
ceases and leaves the body, the spirit goes along with
it. It is also the activity that integrates the mind and
body, connects them, and moves them in the same
direction. You are already breathing anyway, so why
not do so in a way that awakens and integrates your
mind, body, and spirit. It requires no special equip-
ment or expertise.

Other breath practices can be used for various purposes. Breathing can carry away toxins and heal the
body, energize the nervous system, cleanse the lungs
and blood, open intuition, inhibit pain, and heal the
self and others (distance healing). *The Science of Breath*
by Yogi Ramacharaka gives detailed information on
each of these breathing practices. In this section I have
included breathing exercises for healing the emotions.

VISUALIZATION AND IMAGERY

When all things that you see, see you with love,
then all things that you love, soon you will see.

—Melita Denning and Osborne Phillips,
Creative Visualization

MANY BOOKS ON SPIRITUALITY talk about visualization, suggesting that we create our realities through visualization. It is much like prayer. We create and manifest what we pray for, intentionally. We also create what we visualize and the process goes on either intentionally or unintentionally. We create our lives through our conscious, subconscious, and unconscious thoughts and feeling projections.

Some people say, "I can't visualize." Not to worry, we will be including all of the senses in the act of imagery. You may not see a picture, but you may have an inner dialogue or a physical sense in the body. All of these sensations are included in what we call *imagery*. We create what we hold in all of our senses.

This gives us a great responsibility. We create situations in our lives based on our expectations more than on our desires. If you want a new home but do not believe you will find one, the belief carries a lot of weight in your creation. You can be very busy, going through the motions to find a home. You can even be too busy to notice the feelings of unworthiness that are emanating from inside yourself. Busyness often is a way to ignore the painful feelings inside the self.

Look at what is going on inside, because that is what is driving your creations. If you desire a house but feel unworthy of finding one, then the feelings of unworthiness may be a stronger source of creation than your desire. Do not be discouraged. The situation may be there to show you that there are feelings of unworthiness that must be cleared away before you can create from your desire.

What is the driver? Feelings. You can affirm that every condition in life is positive, but if you are feeling pessimistic when you do so, then your affirmations are not charged with the fuel to drive them into existence. When you go to work on an empty stomach, that is like trying to move a car without a driver: There is no positive energy behind the wish to manifest it into a reality. If you are making your wish all the while feeling that you do not deserve to get the wish, then you are manifesting being undeserving. You did not expect to receive your wish and might not even know it if it sat beside you at your kitchen table. You are not filling your wishes with spirit. Spirit includes all the positive, expectant, and charged feelings you can imagine.

Decide what you want, state it as though you already have it, and charge the wish with positive feelings. If you are not feeling positive about your wish, then generate a positive emotion about anything. Use a past positive memory: think of a past success or of someone you love. Send the thought of the memory out, like a prayer, with positive energy. Release it and then expect a return. Open yourself to spiritual guidance and a return on your wish. Be patient. Remember not to shut down if it does not happen now. Keep your spiritual door open and expect a miracle. Project that wish to the universe and know that it is yours. In the meantime, keep clearing the static from your screen. It clears the path for you to see what your spirit is bringing you and eliminates the blocks to receiving it.

There are two basic schools of thought about visualization and projection for yourself and others. Both schools of thought begin with a desire to manifest something in your life. First, you need to get in touch with your desire. What is it that you want? Be sure your wish is in harmony with the highest good. That does not mean you cannot ask for things for yourself, like a job or a car to get to work. Just remember the ripple effect of your wish and be sure it is a wish for a positive outcome. This is important because it helps to eliminate any fear or guilt from entering into the wish. These negative emotions, fear and guilt, interfere with manifestation.

In the first school of thought, you will find literature that tells you to be as specific as possible about your wish. According to this school of thought, if you want a car, you should get a picture of the exact car you want, put it where you will see it, and affirm that you have it. You should feel the way you will feel when you get it. Since the thought and prayer are positively emotionally charged, the laws of attraction should draw your desire toward you. Florence Scovel Shinn's book *Your Word Is Your Wand* offers a number of highly positive affirmations in her book. It can give you a lot of ideas about how to use the words and feelings as positive prayers.

The second school of thought suggests that you ask only for the highest and the best in every situation and leave the specifics up to the higher power. "God Knows Best" would be the motto here. This method suggests that infinite intelligence has a plan for you that is better than the one you can make for yourself. Just identify the need that you have, but do not be specific about how it should come to you. Perhaps you will find merit in both approaches to visualization or imagery.

You are a spark of divine intelligence, so many of your desires are the desires of your soul. These are thoughts that awaken you to your purpose in life. The old saying, "God helps those who help themselves," is telling you to act on divine inspiration. It tells you to sit in meditation to receive the inspiration and to act on it. This suggests a certain amount of visualization and creation of ideas on an active conscious level. The second step is to turn the whole thing over to a higher power. This is known as "letting go and letting God." This is the part where you have received inspiration and acted on it, and now you render the outcome to divine intelligence.

In visualization practice, you actually combine both approaches. You visualize, project your visualizations through positive affirmation and prayer, charge them with positive belief, and let them go to manifest. If this is part of your spiritual purpose, it will manifest. If not, there will be lessons and wisdom to be gained, thoughtful detachment to practice, or emotional feelings to work through. Regardless of the outcome you will have progressed along the spiritual path. Be patient with yourself and keep on digging. There's a treasure chest at the bottom.

MUSIC AND SOUND

Music is the mediator between the life of the spirit and the life of the senses.

—Ludwig Van Beethoven

NOTICE WHAT SOUNDS YOU are taking in. The power of sound is an incredible influence and creates either positive or destructive energy in your life. Watch what you are taking in because sound is not only entered through the ears, but through every pore in your body and in the energy field around the body. Accepting these influences in your life and committing to accept and use them is a way of committing to yourself.

Sound and music are powerful forces that affect our energies. Music, in particular, has a very strong influence on energy. Often, we play music in the car or at home without really paying attention to it, but music will enter the vibratory field of the body and affect our mood, emotions, and health. Music played in major keys lifts you into the spiritual realm, while minor key music draws energy into the physical (Andrews, 1996). Gregorian Chant, which carries a high spiritual vibration, is healing to the mind and body. Among monks who decreased their singing of the chants, declines in health were recorded. The sounds connect to energy centers in the body, primarily through the endocrine glands and spine. Distribution of the energy occurs through the nervous and circulatory systems.

A connection also occurs between sound and color in that the colors of the rainbow are correlated with notes on the scale, and specific places in the body, with each note producing an effect similar to the color energies. In general, the colors of the rainbow—red, orange, yellow, green, blue, indigo, and violet—match with the notes on the scale.

Timing in music also can create effects in the body. For this reason, disharmonious music should be avoided because it will overly ground your energy and even send destructive patterns into the nervous system. Music by George Winston, Paul Winter, and other musicians which does not have a specific number of beats to the measure, but flows without form, is highly beneficial to health and relaxation. Music in an even timing tends to regulate your body to the timing of the music rather than allow it to regulate itself.

Music and sound have neurobiological effects on the body that either strengthen and improve physical and emotional functioning or work against the healthy balance of the body. In addition, music and sound actually change the neurological response of the brain. These changes may produce emotional reactions, resulting in chemical changes in the body. Note that the changes can occur immediately in the physiology or may occur in the brain and create a resulting response in the body.

Sound vibrations actually move through skin and bones, which act as conductors for the sounds. For this reason, certain jobs have noise limits and limits on the number of hours that individuals can work at them. Much research has been done in order to determine the effects of this biological phenomenon. When positive sounds were played, results indicated improvements in the amount of milk that cows would give, increased rates of learning, improvement in bread rising, and ability to reduce certain medications. These specific studies involved the use of Mozart's music. Evidence of music as a substitute for medicine occurred as early as 1741, when Johann Sebastian Bach was commissioned to write the Goldberg variations. These variations included thirty harpsichord pieces, which relaxed the mind and created a cure for insomnia. Jane Stanley, a music therapist at Florida State University, found that music enhanced physicians' objectives with patients, both physically and emotionally. Although music cannot be used as a substitute for medical treatment or medication, it appears to be able to enhance the effects of medical treatments, and in some cases, even permits for a reduction in the amount of medication required.

Music can even be used before surgery to allow a patient to associate the music with a positive state of health and relaxation. The music is then used during the surgery and after to create the same sense of relaxation and freedom from stress. Auditory nerves remain alert during anesthesia, and some patients have needed less anesthesia when Mozart's music was played. Patients may even experience less symptoms during chemotherapy with the use of Mozart's music. The ear acts as a messenger to the mind, body, and emotions. It is like an herb, or medicine, and has a similar effect as beautiful art has to the eyes. The air is the carrier of this positive benefit like the bases that are used in pills or herbs. In Don Campbell's work *The Mozart Effect,* many of these effects are explained in great detail.

We must begin to take note of the effects that sounds have upon us. Surrounding yourself with a diet of healthy music, is very much the same as breathing clean air, drinking clean water, and eating healthy foods. Our body, mind, and emotions respond to the effects of music or sound. Some classical music allows the mind to rest and sleep, while other classical compositions awaken higher levels of creativity. Your intent and purpose should influence your choice of musical selections. Steven Halpern has produced a number of different audiotapes and compact discs, which can be used to create various reactions in the mind, body, and emotions. Belleruth Naperstek has created a series of audio tapes which can be used to assist with the healing of various physical conditions. Belleruth combines voice with music on her tapes, and research has shown that they are highly effective.

Color

Colors have a strong influence on our mood and energy level. You do not even have to be taking in the color through your eyes in order to be affected by it. Blind people have been taught to discern colors of fabric simply by holding them in their hand. They can discern whether the colors are warm (red, gold, orange, and yellow) or cool (blue, green, turquoise, white, and silver). With increased training and sensitivity, they can even discern the warm colors from one another, red from gold and orange from yellow. The same levels of sensitivity can be obtained by sighted individuals, but the blind studies document and show that color energies can be perceived through the hands and the physical body. This means that the colors are having their effect whether we are paying attention to them or not.

Choose colors wisely because they significantly effect your energy level. In general, warm colors tend to increase energy levels and be more stimulating. Yellow is an excellent color for stimulating mental activity, so if you are writing on yellow legal pads, this is excellent. Red tends to energize and then exhaust, much in the same way as caffeine. It gives you initial stimulation and an energizing effect, but in the long term, wearing a lot of red may become exhausting. Cool colors are extremely good for relaxation and healing because they calm you. Blue and green are very calming and healing colors, and are particularly good to have around for someone who is going through a healing process. White, pale yellow, and gold are highly spiritual colors and would be excellent for a meditation area. Pastels in general are positive because they contain white. If you like earth tones, they should be used in moderation, because too much dark brown, rust, and tan are too grounding. If you need to feel more grounded, a little bit of earth tones will go a long way. Green, blue, and lilac mimic nature and are positive colors to use to raise spiritual energy.

Be conscious of the colors you wear closest to your body and those you keep in your home, car, and workplace. These colors are affecting you without your awareness. The color of your car interior, for example, is the color that surrounds you, and to which you are exposed for many hours a week. Choose a color that will produce the effects you desire. When in need, visualizing a particular color around you can be especially useful. Use blue if you are trying to calm down, gold to stimulate mental activity, gold and white to surround and protect yourself.

If at any time you become too uncomfortable during this exercise, stop. Imagine yourself in a place where you feel completely safe and secure. If you do not have a memory of having been in such a secure place, create one in your imagination before you begin the exercise. In this way, if material becomes too disturbing, you can go to the safe place you have created for yourself and stay there until you feel more relaxed.

Exercise: Color Breathing for Healing

Goal: To use color to assist the healing process.

1. Choose a color you feel would be healing for you today. If you are unsure, the following list will show the effects on the body and mind of certain colors.

Blue: calm	Purple: self-mastery
Green: healing	Pale yellow: mind stimulating
Pale pink: love	Violet: rising above situations
White: pure spirituality	

Note: Red, black, orange, and intense colors are not recommended for color breathing.

2. Think about any feelings of upset, anger, tension, or other negative emotions that you have now. Stop and notice where in your body you feel the tension. Right now, think about a time when you were distressed or think about something that is upsetting to you in general. Notice where in your body you feel the discomfort. Then, with your eyes closed, begin to breathe, imagining the breath moving to the specific

part of your body where the negative emotions
are felt. Then exhale and allow the tension to
leave your body through your breath. Now, add
a color to the breath. Think about a color that
feels particularly healing, calming, and relaxing
to you today. You may imagine pink, purple,
gold, white, blue, or green, or another color
that feels relaxing to you and healing at this
moment. Now imagine that the breath is this
color. Breathe down into the place in your body
where you feel the tension, and then release it
out through your breath. Again, continuing to
breathe into the place in the body where the
tension is felt, visualizing the breath in the healing color that you desire to use today. Continue
this process for several minutes if necessary,
until you begin to feel that healing is taking
place.

The beneficial effects of smell and touch also should
not be ignored. The fine sciences of aromatherapy,
massage therapy, healing touch, Reiki, and therapeutic touch are excellent practices for Spiritual Fitness. The resources at the end of the chapter can
guide you in your exploration of smell and touch.

SPIRITUAL FITNESS TRANSFORMATION
THROUGH MOVEMENT

As I have surrendered to the . . . embrace of the
dance, I've found a language of patterns I can trust
to deliver us into eternal truths, truths older than
time.

—Gabrielle Roth, *Sweat Your Prayers*

MOVEMENT AS WELL AS touch in a kinesthetic sense is
intricately linked with the enhancement of spiritual
energy. Movement systems such as yoga, tai chi, and
chi kung not only benefit all of the physical systems of
the body but balance and uplift the spiritual energy of
the body. Gabrielle Roth, in *Sweat Your Prayers,* shows
us how different forms of dance and movement can
release energies in a way that is beneficial for health.
For a more detailed explanation of these energy systems and the way in which they affect health, see Carolyn Myss' *Energy Anatomy.* If you are a particularly
kinesthetic individual, movement systems will tap into
your primary representational system, and you will feel
very comfortable with them. If you are heavily oriented
toward visual or auditory learning modalities, then
kinesthetic activities would help to balance you and
open up your kinesthetic sense. I recommend that you
add movement to your *daily practice* in order to assist
with Spiritual Fitness in your body, mind, and emotions. We will address movement activities, which will
be highly beneficial, next.

I woke up one morning at the Himalayan International Institute in the usual fashion. Usual meant a small, bare room with no television or radio and, certainly, no chocolate. I was attending a weeklong training program for therapists who use holistic methods in their practices. On the fourth day of the program, after herbal tea, participants moved in meditative silence to the yoga room, where we stretched in intermediate yoga postures for one hour. I returned to my room to shower and glanced in the mirror, did a double take, and stared back at my wide-eyed image. I looked younger than I had before the class. The oxygen that had been channeled through my body during yoga had brightened my face! My mind went to my aunt in her seventies, a lifelong practitioner of yoga, who still went to the beach in her bikini. Clearly, there was something to the link between yoga and maintaining youthfulness.

I had read Jess Stearn's work about yoga and youth and was inspired. Yoga relaxes the muscles and massages the inner organs. There are yoga exercises to stimulate the health of specific body systems, organs, emotional conditions, and energy forces in the body. This vital energy has many different names in different cultures. In eastern medicine, these energy systems are based on the flow of *prana*—a yoga term to describe the vital life force energy. In Chinese, it is called *Chi,* in Japanese, it is *Ki.* Western medicine borrows these terms because it does not have a name for it! Life force energy treatments are not a part of the traditional medical treatments.

This life force energy is intricately connected to, and moved by, the breath. Since tension is inevitable in life and tensions block the flow of life force energy, diseases occur. Yoga naturally releases the tensions, allowing the energy to flow again. It is like releasing a knot from the garden hose and letting the water flow freely again. Once the energy is flowing normally, the body rebalances and heals itself. So often we are too busy to pay attention to our bodies, or to even notice where we are blocked or tense. In my experience, I have been able to regain my emotional balance after fifteen minutes of yoga, even following a day of work that left me emotionally out of sorts. Based on my personal success with yoga, I studied it as much as possible and began leading classes for adults and children. I witnessed the physical and emotional healing that was supported by yoga exercise. Some of the exercises even helped to facilitate a meditative state. I remember teaching yoga classes and getting into meditative yoga postures. There were times I shifted into meditation and had to bring myself back. In the meantime, my class would be holding a posture and waiting for my return.

Often emotions become locked in the tissues of the body. They can become buried and cause physical problems that have no obvious explanation. At times, while receiving massage and other types of bodywork, I have

had vivid memories of events form my past. During recollection of these memories, I felt the emotions as
intensely as when I first experienced them. When the
body worker is skilled and compassionate, the old
memory can be released and healed. A similar process
occurs in yoga, Tai Chi, and Chi Kung. Instead of stor-
ing emotion in the body, creating emotional blocks, the
breathing and stretching exercises release the feelings
and allow them to be processed. Feelings of rejection,
worry, anger, loss, and confusion, whether we are aware
of them or we suppress them, affect our bodies and
cause blocks to health. Lack of exercise builds up tension, creating blocks in the nervous system, circulatory
system, lymphatic system, and the energy system of the
body. If we add more tension through poor diet, drugs,
or alcohol, we need to exercise even more.

When the energy is flowing, we have a flow of "Chi"
which allows for a greater balance of Yin-Yang elements. These are the masculine and feminine halves
of every personality. They represent the opposites in
the personality: Darkness and light, activity and pas-
sivity, black and white, male and female, hot and cold.
It is healthier to live in the gray area where we have a
balance of each. Movement forms such as yoga assist
us in balanced living and are especially helpful if our
lives are over- or underactive.

At times when we are problem-solving, we may
either become lethargic and hopeless or overactive and
aggressive about getting to a solution. These are imbal-

ances in the "Chi" or Yin-Yang energy. Yoga is a good technique for balancing because it raises lethargic energy and calms and slows overactive energy. In other words, yoga can be helpful with either feelings and symptoms of anxiety, as well as those of depression.

Other forms of movement have similar effects, such as "Tai Chi," and "Chi Kung." Gabrielle Roth in *Sweat Your Prayers* shares the importance of dance: "I feel my soul and my body when I dance . . . I've surrendered to the wild, ecstatic embrace of the dance, I've found a language of patterns I can trust to deliver . . . into eternal truths . . . older than time. In the rhythm of the body, we can trace our holiness, roots that go all the way back . . ."

This doesn't mean that jogging, aerobics, and weightlifting, the more common forms of exercise, are not beneficial to health. The movement exercises I have discussed are especially a part of Spiritual Fitness. They feed the mind, body, and spirit. It is good to have some type of spiritual movement practice when you are on the path. Remember that the spirit is the source of all health and abundance which brings us to our healthiest and fullest selves.

Encouragement Notes

- You now have many of the basics of Spiritual
  Fitness. You have a prayer statement that you
  can add to as you have more positive spiritual
  experiences. You have an understanding of
  breathing, movement, colors, and sounds and
  how you can use them for your Spiritual Fitness.
  You have let go of some old limiting beliefs and
  trances and you continue to release them more
  as time passes. You have positive affirmations to
  reflect your new consciously chosen trances. You
  know what levels of consciousness you want to
  focus on to enhance your growth.

- Add to your *daily practices* some of the techniques from this chapter. After your prayer
  statement and positive affirmations, do a
  breathing exercise to calm and quiet your mind.
  Or do color breathing if you have something
  you want to heal. This should bring your *daily
  practice* to about fifteen minutes. This excludes
  the time you spend doing the exercises in the
  book or any physical Spiritual Fitness exercises
  you may have chosen to do. You may want to do
  physical exercises at another time if you cannot
  manage a large enough block of time at your
  daily practice time. If you prefer to exercise with
  your *daily practice*, do the physical exercise at the
  beginning.

- Notice all the sounds, manmade and natural, in
  your environment. Be aware of traffic noise,

music in stores and restaurants, people's voices, etc. Notice how each of these sounds makes you feel. Now you are in a position to choose what is best for you.

- Make conscious choices of color in your clothes, houses, and field of vision. You can now choose to have the healing benefits of the colors that are best for you.

- Begin to take deep breaths at times of the day when you notice your first symptom of stress occurring. This is the one you identified from your own awareness or from the symptom list. Be aware that your body is effectively telling you it is time to relax your nervous symptom. When you notice the symptom, do not become upset that it is there, but be grateful that you know it is time to take deep breaths! Take breaths deeply and diaphragmatically until you have reduced or eliminated your symptom.

- You are more than halfway through your Spiritual Fitness training!

RESOURCES FOR CHAPTER THREE

Books

The Seven Spiritual Laws of Success. Deepak Chopra, Amber-Allen, San Rafael, CA, 1994.

Science of Breath. Yogi Ramacharaka, Yogi Publication Society: Chicago, 1904.

Sweat Your Prayers. Gabrielle Roth, Jeremy Tarcher: NY, 1997.

Yoga, Youth, & Reincarnation. Jess Stearn, Valley of the Sun Publishing: Malibu, CA, 1993.

Bioenergetics. Alexander Lowen, M.D., Penguin Books: NY, 1981.

Three Magic Words. U. S. Andersen, Wilshire: N. Hollywood, CA, 1964.

The Game of Life and How to Play It. Florence Scovel Shinn, DeVorss: Marina Del Ray, CA, 1925.

Music

Johann Sebastian Bach, *The Goldberg Variations*

Stephen Halpern, *Spectrum Suite*

Suzanne Ciani, *The Private Music of Suzanne Ciani*

Enya, *Watermark*

American Gramaphone, *Sunday Morning Coffee*

4

Meditation and Prayer

Prayer is talking to God . . . meditation is listening for a response.

—Anthony Campolo,
author and minister

Riches You Will Gain from This Chapter

- Awareness of the different perspectives on prayer
- Addition of prayer to your daily practice
- Addition of meditation to your daily practice

IF BREATHING IS THE foundation of any spiritual program, then prayer and meditation are the heart and soul of it. When I had the opportunity to hear Christian minister Anthony Campolo speak, I found him to be most passionate in his views, often sparking controversy and provoking thoughtful discussions.

He had a television show in which he sat in a coffee shop and debated religious philosophy with another minister. I will never forget how Dr. Campolo compared the process of prayer and meditation to that of a telephone conversation: prayer is the part of the conversation where you call God and tell Him all you want to say. The problem is that most people then hang up and break the connection. You would never do that in conversation with anyone else. You would listen to their reflections in return. Meditation is that part of communication where you listen for God's response to your prayers.

PERSPECTIVES ON PRAYER

Pray without ceasing.

—1 Thessalonians 5:17

YOU CAN LIVE AS if everything is a prayer, calling in each
movement and thought to greater spiritual expression. But, when you pray aloud, are you talking to
God? Do you talk to Allah? To Jesus? To Buddha? Or
do you call upon that universal divine mind intelligence of which we are all a part? The infinite divine
energy is the power source that fuels all our souls and
allows us to shine in our individual world. In other
words, we are the gods of our own universe, sparks of
divinity that are all connected to the universal source.
Certainly, at times, we will pray to specific masters,
angels, or saints, but much of our prayer is directed to
infinite intelligence or God. If we have been doing our
personal work and have been clearing our perceptual
screens of static, we begin to gain glimpses of this
divine light. You can see your car windshield more
clearly once it is free of debris. The view of God is the
same.

In St. Theresa of Avila's *Interior Castles,* the castles,
or mansions, represent levels of our conscious understanding of God. St. Theresa of Avila was a sixteenth-
century nun. She believed that she had no talent for
writing, and she humbly denied having the intelligence to even do so. Having been directed by her supe-
riors to write, however, she wrote of the mansions in a

manner which showed a clarity of vision of the places where "the most secret things pass between God and the soul." The process describes "the course of the mystical life, the soul's progress from the first mansion to the seventh. This transformation moves us from the beginning levels of understanding of God into creatures who become the brides of the spiritual marriage. The door by which we enter each castle is prayer and meditation."

The levels of awareness represented by each of the seven mansions are progressive. In mansion one, the souls have many attachments to the outside world. They then progress through humility to mansion two, where they attend to every possible opportunity for advancement for the soul. (This is much like the desire that brought you to your search for Spiritual Fitness.) In mansion three, the soul has attained a high level of virtue, but can still fall back. In mansion three, the soul may be disposed to many acts of charity, but has not yet experienced the full force of love and is still governed by reason.

By the time we reach the fourth mansion, the supernatural element of mystical life occurs. In the fifth mansion, the soul is fully possessed by God, leading to the betrothal of the soul to God in the sixth mansion. In mansion seven, the spiritual marriage occurs. No higher state can be attained while on earth.

Through St. Theresa's beautifully written book, you can feel her fire for connection with God in much the same way as our own. Her life of devotion to the path has given us the exquisite metaphors of *Interior Castles.*

It is no coincidence that we see the number "7" across many religious belief systems. In Carolyn Myss' book *Anatomy of the Spirit,* she parallels the seven Christian sacraments with the seven Sefirot of the Jewish faith, and the seven chakras, or energy centers of the body, in Eastern religion. This shows us that the path of the seven levels is universal to many philosophies on spiritual development. We see that each of these religions had a glimpse of God that was similar, but somewhat personalized and based on individual cultures, thus reminding us that the truth of God is universal.

In *Anatomy of the Spirit,* we are guided through the seven levels represented by the chakras. The first, located at the base of the spine, is related to the material world (beginning to sound familiar?). The second, located at the spleen, is related to sex and physical desire. The third chakra brings lessons of the ego and self-esteem, and is located in the solar plexus. The fourth chakra is about love and is located in the heart. In the fifth chakra, we deal with self-expression (at the throat, naturally), and in the sixth, lessons of insight, wisdom, and intuition. The sixth level is located just above the eyes in the area known as the "third eye." At the seventh chakra, on the top of the head, we deal with spirituality on a pure level. Imbalances at any of these levels can cause health problems related to the part of the body where the chakra is located. Again, we see the connectedness of our mind, body, and spirit.

Each chakra parallels one of the seven sacraments, says Myss. During the Christian sacrament of Baptism, we receive God's grace; at Communion, that grace represents holy union with God and others; then in Confirmation, a reception of grace that enhances self-esteem occurs (as before with the solar plexus chakra). Marriage is compared to the heart chakra. Here, we must recognize the need to love ourselves so that we can fully love another. In confession, at the throat chakra, we have an extremely powerful opportunity to call back to ourselves our own spiritual power. This can be one of the most life-changing experiences of transformation if we take responsibility for seeing all the places where we gave our power away.

I used to think confession was an uncomfortable experience of having to tell your sins to a stranger in the confessional booth. In Myss' view, our "sins" are the times we gave our power away. These are the times when we said: "If I only had more money, I could be happy." "If only my mate would love me the way my parents never did, then I could be healed." "If only I had a better job, then I could feel better about myself." Confession is about reclaiming our power for our own happiness and balance and atoning for the times when we gave it away.

Ordination, at the sixth chakra, is an opportunity to receive grace to make your path of service sacred. Finally, Extreme Unction, or last rites at the seventh chakra, allows us to finish our business, allows us to love in this dimension and in the next.

We then can compare the chakras and sacraments to the Sefirot of the Tree of Life of the Jewish Kaballah. The Sefirot are considered the blueprints or qualities that God shares with man. They are spiritual powers that develop and refine us in our journey.

We can see that there are many paths of religious adherence and many ways to pray. If we see that each path leads to God and that our creations are reflections of this understanding and of our progress on the path, we can take back our spiritual power.

PRAYER RESEARCH

"He's got the whole world in his hands, he's got the whole wide world in his hands/He's got you and me in his hands, he's got everybody in his hands."

—African American Spiritual

DR. LARRY DOSSEY IS a medical doctor and former cochair of Mind-Body Interventions panel for the National Institute of Health. Dr. Dossey conducted scientific research on the effectiveness of prayer. These were not acts of faith, but instead were attempts to validate, in a concrete scientific way, whether prayer actually had an effect on the person who was prayed for. How it affects us, we may not know, but the goal of the research was if it affects us.

Because of Dr. Dossey and his colleagues, we know that prayer is as legitimate a part of a treatment plan as medication. In *Prayer Is Good Medicine,* he states that if Jesus, Mohammed, and Buddha had penicillin, they probably would have used it, along with prayer. The evidence clearly suggests that when people are prayed for, they heal faster and with fewer complications. When we move to the section on visualization, we can actually learn tools for praying for ourselves very specifically and in more complete ways.

Dossey's results make it clear that prayer works. He also states that, "No specific religion has a monopoly on prayer." This may conflict with religious beliefs that hold that their prayers or members of their religion are the only ones who can reach God effectively. Dossey proves that the opposite is true. Groups or individuals who claim exclusive contact with the divine, place themselves in a special status which they truly cannot claim. Dr. Dossey says, "Prayer experiments level the playing field. They show that prayer is a universal phenomena belonging to every faith . . . and these studies affirm tolerance."

Dr. Dossey is not the only person to complete research on prayer. The results of a study done by Dr. Franklin Loehr, a Presbyterian minister and scientist, showed that even plant seeds respond to prayer. Positive prayer resulted in faster germination and more vigorous plants. Negative prayer halted or suppressed growth of the seeds *(Scientific Research of Prayer: Can the*

Power of Prayer Be Proven, Debra Williams). Dr. Daniel Benor found that the growth of fungus was influenced by prayer at great distances *(Complementary Medical Research* 4:1, 1990). Gregg Braden in *Walking Between the Worlds: The Science of Compassion* (1997) presents a case that human emotion affects the actual patterning of the genetic material DNA. With important implications, subjects were able to alter the genetic mutation rate of bacteria. It suggests that we can in fact alter conditions, which are predisposed genetically.

Further studies at Duke University found that people who were prayed for had a 50 percent reduction in heartbeat abnormalities and a 100 percent reduction in heart attacks and heart failure. These results were even greater than the positive results achieved through some of the imagery and therapeutic touch, which were 20 to 30 percent reductions. But does a lack of spiritual commitment cause reverse effects in health? In studies at John Hopkins Medical School on the disease of alcoholism in medical students, the strongest predictor of developing the disease was a lack of religious affiliation. Even church attendance had lower rates of depression and anxiety than nonattendees in a study at the National Institute of Mental Health. Among the 720 study participants, the higher the church attendance, the lower the psychopathology.

Elaine Gottlieb reports about the healing power of positive emotions in *The Power of Prayer in Healing.* She reviews studies done with videotapes of Mother Teresa.

After viewing the tapes showing Mother Teresa lovingly caring for her patients, saliva antibodies showed increases in immune function in viewers.

Some religious groups oppose calling positive intention prayer by saying that positive intention is not prayer. But what is positive intention? Isn't it holding a state of mind of unconditional positive acceptance? The thoughts of such acceptance and love appear to be prayers when directed toward cells, people or plants, according to the studies. It comes from the highest and best part of you. Constant prayer is even possible once you reach a state of God consciousness in which God is an inescapable constant in your mind. This state of mind seems more effective than prayers said mindlessly or without focused caring about the recipients. The research suggests that our intention is the driving force behind the prayer. If you say kind words to someone, but inside harbor jealousy, your intention determines the outcome. We can usually sense when people are genuine.

Deepak Chopra, in *How to Know God,* tells us that intention includes your highest vision. "If you set your intention toward God, spirit grows . . . Once you plant the seed of intention, your soul's journey unfolds automatically." The desire to feel God's presence in your life and to have a life of meaning are some of the basic intentions that mark a spiritual life. Dr. Chopra recommends knowing your spiritual intentions and allowing God to take over. In this way we give up the need for power and control, two needs that separate us from God.

In Dossey's studies, when people were prayed for in specific ways, without their knowledge, they healed more rapidly than those in control groups for whom no prayers were said. Distance did not matter; prayers from across the country were as effective as those from across the street. No physical energy has ever been detected passing between the healer and the healed in these studies. If you are interested, quantum physics offers explanations of these effects that are discussed by Dr. Dossey and by Dr. Deepak Chopra in *Quantum Physics*. I would encourage you to look into these readings if you are interested in the physical/spiritual explanations.

Physicians training medical students at Duke University are now encouraged to be holistically well themselves before they try to heal their patients. The soul of medicine is saying "Physician, heal thyself." ("Returning Soul to Medicine," Gail Bernice Holland, *IONS Review*, Sept. 2002.) When doctors are enthusiastic about their recommendations, and follow their own advice, patients are more likely to adhere to treatment, and to show greater improvements. Overall, the research of prayer and thoughts is changing the face of medical practice.

Be aware that your thought energy affects the energy of the entire world. As we think, pray, speak, and believe, we create our worlds. Our thoughts and feelings do touch others, and we do create change. Because of this, we need to evolve and shift perceptions as deeply as possible. The higher the thoughts we send out continually, the more we affect others in positive ways. Our thoughts are like prayers. They are felt by those of whom we think. We can choose to think of others in lack and limitation or see them as the highest and best that they can be. Consider the expression, "You catch more flies with honey." This applies not only to our actions, but to our thoughts.

When we hold others in a positive light, we not only send that thought out as a prayer, but we treat that person as a positive person and expect the best from them. Have you noticed that when you appreciated someone's behavior, the behavior was repeated? If you tell one of your children, "I like how you've cleaned your room without having to be told," aren't they likely to do it again? But if you pay attention to the messy room and nag your children, saying, "Why don't you ever clean your room?" you have just characterized them as individuals who do not clean their rooms. This becomes a part of their self-concept.

Whether we pray for others by holding them in our thoughts in positive ways or project through our words, we are using forms of prayer. Growing up, I did not understand the saying, "Worry is a prayer for a thing you do not want," but now I do. When we worry we are consciously picturing problems. They become accepted by our mind as realities in our self-concepts.

We, and those around us, are influenced by our own thoughts and feeling projections. What's more, we influence our lives with our conscious, subconscious, and unconscious thoughts. What? Just when we have started controlling our conscious thoughts, we have to be responsible for the subconscious and unconscious ones? Yes. And the more we evolve, meditate, pray, pay attention to our dreams, and do the work to heal our emotions, the more we can bring to consciousness these hidden beliefs. Many of these beliefs will have to be released so that we can make room for so much more. In the final chapter, we will discuss a rocky, powerful part of my own spiritual journey in which these beliefs came to the surface in ways I could never have imagined. When we pray for change, healing can rip from us the very foundations we once lived from in ignorance and take us into a whole new and higher place.

HOW TO PRAY

All that we are is a result of what we have thought,
so think as if every thought were to be etched in
fire upon the sky for all and everything to see,
   So speak as if the entire world were but a single
ear intent on hearing what you have to say,
   So do as if every deed were to recoil upon your
head,
   So wish as if you were the wish.

                                        — Buddha

HOW DO WE PRAY? First, you are already using your
prayer statement to begin your *daily practice*. This is a
statement of a positive spiritual experience, which
recalls feelings of connectedness with the universal
spirit. What then? Do we need certain prayers? We can
use positive, affirmative prayers that state the conditions we desire in our lives and hearts. These can be
found in the Bible, the Torah, the Koran, and Kab-
balah, in prayer books by modern mystics, and in our
own self-created prayers. We do not have to create new
ones if we do not want to, at least not until we feel
comfortable just speaking from the heart. I especially
like the Twenty-third Psalm, because it states so positively that we have all of God's gifts:

> The Lord is my shepherd, I shall not want. He
> makes me lie down in green pastures. He leads me
> beside still waters. He restores my soul. He leads
> me in paths of righteousness for His name's sake.
> Yea, though I walk through the valley of the
> shadow of death, I would fear no evil, for Thou art
> with me. Thy rod and Thy staff, they comfort me.

Thou preparest a table before me in the presence
of mine enemies. Thou anointest my head with
oil. My cup runneth over. Surely, goodness and
mercy shall follow me all the days of my life and I
will dwell in the House of the Lord, forever.

The prayer does not say, "Please give me green pastures," or "Please restore my soul." It says, "God restores
my soul. He gives me green pastures." We see ourselves
as having these things, not as wanting them. This is an
important distinction. We do not need to pray that we
continue wanting; we need to pray that we have what
we need.

Exercise: Daily Prayer

Goal: Adding prayers to your daily practice.

1. After your beginning prayer statement, add a
   few prayers that you like. These can be prayers
   from other sources or statements of affirmation
   that you write for yourself. This is the part of
   your *daily practice* where you are talking to God.
   After your selected prayers, just speak to God
   from the heart in an affirmative way. Be sure to
   involve your thoughts and your feelings. Your
   thoughts are the car and the feelings are the driver. As Lynn Grabhorn says in *Excuse Me, Your
   Life Is Waiting,* unless you can create an intense
   level of emotion and feel in the moment what
   you will feel when your prayers are answered,
   you can not drive the prayer.

2. Next address your "healing list." This is the list that contains the names of loved ones for whom you want to pray. Address their prayer needs for health, employment, or whatever assistance they need. Then move on to prepare for meditation.

MEDITATION

Always seek the guidance and good judgement of spiritual light and understanding.

—Unity School of Christianity

THE MIND IS OFTEN like an undisciplined child, bouncing from place to place and thought to thought without a focus. In Buddhism, this is referred to as "Monkey Mind." Until you release some of the activity of your mind, you are not able to meditate.

For the first month of your meditation practice, you can do the following exercise that will prepare you for meditation. You can also do this exercise any time you want to clear your mind of stressful thoughts or prepare to sleep or for meditation. I call the exercise "Mind washing." This exercise is done for about twenty minutes at the end of the day for the first month. Then it can be done for a brief period before each meditation. It will clear your mind and allow for a deeper meditation experience. "Mind washing" also has many healing benefits. It releases your thoughts so that your nervous system can relax and your body can heal. It also has the effect of giving you detachment from problems. This will carry over into everyday life. You may find that occurrences that used to get you very upset will bother you less. This detachment allows you to remain far more balanced and, as a result, more centered in your spirit. It allows you to be less effected by outside events in your life or other's lives.

This is one of the keys to Spiritual Fitness: remaining in your spirit and keeping the spirit in the driver's seat of life. It is the spirit that can observe your mental activity, emotional responses, and physical sensations. During this exercise, you will get a sense of being in your spirit, because you will notice that there is a part of you that observes the other three parts of your self. You may be excited about beginning meditation practice at this point, and want to begin it immediately, but know that once you do the "Mind washing" process, you will have a deeper meditation experience.

Exercise: Mind Washing

Goal: To release thoughts and experience detachment from them.

Sit in your meditation area. Visualize in your mind that you are sitting in front of a beautiful ocean. You can see the surroundings in any way that you want to, with seagulls, sunshine, palm trees, or anything else that allows you to feel calm. Then, begin allowing your thoughts to rise. As soon as a thought becomes conscious, and as soon as you are aware that you are having a thought or feeling of any kind, gently place it on an incoming wave and let it wash away from you. Then see what comes up next.

Do not finish any of the thoughts, do not pay attention to them, do not judge them as good or bad, and do not take time to complete the thought. Just as soon as it comes into consciousness, place it on the wave and let it wash away from you. If you hear sounds in the room, simply observe them, place them on the ocean waves, and let them float away. The same is true for thoughts and feelings: let them come up, place them on the ocean, and let them wash away, very disinterestedly, as though they are not even a part of you, as though they are a seashell, simply unattached to you, washing away into the ocean. Continue allowing each thought to arise and then let it go. See what comes up next. Just observe what is coming up, then release it and let it move away from you onto each ocean wave.

You can do this activity until you feel that you have actually let go of much of what is on your conscious mind. At that time, stop, take a minute to enjoy the feeling of having been cleared of thoughts and feelings, and then move on to your meditation practice. If during this exercise you think, "I'm not doing this right," "I don't know how to do this," "Nothing's coming up," simply place those thoughts on the ocean and let them wash away as well. It may not be easy for you to see or visualize the ocean, but perhaps you can feel yourself there or allow yourself to have a sense of being there by hearing the ocean waves. An ocean wave tape is useful for doing this exercise because it allows you to have a feeling of being there more completely.

There are many ways to meditate. Most of them involve some sort of process of slowing the mind. We might strive to slow our minds to achieve the silence in which we can hear God, or our intuitive guidance. We may want to communicate with angels or other spiritual guides to gain this guidance, and it is quite possible to do so. In other cases, we might meditate to get into the silence so that we can hear nothing. Buddhist meditation is useful for this purpose. Reaching a quiet mind is a way of arriving at your god self; all else, even positive thoughts or guidance, are considered distractions to the process.

Then there is the concept of living meditation or walking meditation, which is the process of living completely in the moment, being fully present. Walking meditation reminds me of the story of the man who met his spiritual teacher on the way to dinner one night. When the student stopped to greet his teacher, he said that he was going to dinner. His teacher said, "I am walking." The student was oriented to his destination, while the teacher was fully in the present.

You may use whatever you are drawn to for your own meditation. I recommend trying several methods and then choosing one to practice. Staying too long in the exploration phase can be a form of not committing to a spiritual path. It may stem from fear. Committing allows us to face these fears.

Try the following exercise to begin a meditation process. To prepare for meditation, you might direct yourself toward the following steps. When you are comfortable with the process, try doing it without the tape or book. When I first started meditating, I meditated at 11 o'clock each night. One night, I was cleaning out the attic and had lost track of the time. At exactly 11 o'clock, my mind and body went into a deep state of meditation and I was forced to stop working! My body and mind were trained and responded to my regular practice.

Exercise: Meditation Practice

Goal: To begin a meditation practice.

1. Choose approximately the same time and place to meditate each day.

2. Bless your entire home the first time you meditate. Bless each door, window, all furnishings, floors, porches, rooms, and the yard. You can use holy water or bless some water yourself to use in the clearing process. Some philosophies, especially Eastern and Christian, also use incense to bless each area of the house. You can use a house blessing prayer, such as the Twenty-third Psalm, or some other positive prayer, as you move through each part of the house, blessing it. It is good to do this practice once a month to rededicate your home and protect it.

3. Take a brief shower. Let the influences of the day wash away. See stress washing out of your energy system and body, mentally and physically, as you shower.

4. Choose your special meditation place, a spot in your home where you only meditate. Dedicate this area to meditation. It can be a special chair or a whole room. If it is a room, be sure that it is uncluttered. On a table or dresser nearby, put articles that make you feel your connection to God. These can be religious items, books, or pictures of spiritual teachers, either living or dead, and other spiritual reminders. Then place a white candle in a glass container, like the ones you light in many churches, in the center of your meditation table. Light the candle each time you meditate.

5. At the beginning of your meditation, find yourself a comfortable place and begin to bring the focus of your mind to your breathing. Observe the breath as it comes and goes—smoothly and evenly, and you can allow the breath to be smooth and even. You may want to gently count the number of seconds that it takes to inhale and the number of seconds that it takes to exhale—now. Good!

6. Make the prayer statement that you have already formed. Say any prayers or affirmations that you have prepared.

7. Now, to begin to relax, slow the breath by one count on the inhale and one count on the

exhale. So if you were breathing in for a count of
two and out for two, make it three now. Allow
the breath to be slower and deeper than before.
Regulating the breath regulates the mind and
the body and brings them into harmony with
one another. Now, each time that you inhale,
feel yourself breathing in feelings of peace and
relaxation and feel this peace and relaxation
moving through your entire body. As you
exhale, feel yourself breathing out tension or
discomfort and feel it dissolve as it leaves your
body. Breathe in peace and relaxation and feel
it flow through the entire body now, exhale tension and feel it dissolve—now.

Now perhaps you can remember a time when
you felt very relaxed, or just imagine one, and
remember how it felt to be relaxed. Remember
what your body experienced and your mind and
your emotions. Remember feeling calm and,
perhaps, you can remember everything that you
could see at that time of relaxation—all of the
colors and forms. Then remember what you
could hear, perhaps even sounds that you had-
n't paid attention to at the time. Just be in this
place for a minute, as you breathe deeply and
evenly—letting go of everything and being here
now, focused in the present, in this place of
relaxation.

Now, let's take a walk in our mind—at the
beach—and feel yourself there now.

8. If there's somewhere else you'd rather be, that's
fine. But, if you can relax at the beach, imagine

what the ocean breeze and the warmth from
the sun feel like. And feel the sand in your toes
as you listen to the waves coming and going,
bringing their energy to you, and carrying away
anything you do not need. And see what color
the water is today, and the sand.

Now, you can allow any distracting thoughts
or concerns to surface on their own, and each
time the ocean wave comes in, place any
thought or concern on the wave and let it be
washed away. Don't concern yourself about
whether the thought is positive or negative,
and don't take any time to decide how you feel
about the thought. Just as soon as it surfaces,
place it on the wave and let it be washed away
from you. And don't be concerned about it or
where it goes. Take some time now to allow the
wave to come in and place any thought on the
wave that comes up and let it wash away from
you, letting go now. Continue to allow the
waves to come in and carry away anything
that surfaces in your mind. If it's something
positive or important, it can come back later.
But we don't even need to decide that now
because your mind knows how to let go completely and to release so that you can relax,
restore, and heal. Continue to let the waves
come in, notice what comes to mind; and then
disinterestedly, just release it, away from you,
letting go, more and more.

Now, let's take a walk on the beach and feel
the easy flowing movement of walking along-

side the water, feeling it come up over your feet
as you look down at them. See the water moving, in and out between your toes, washing away
anything that you don't need as you walk. You
may want to think of a question that you would
like to have answered from within yourself.
Something that's been puzzling or troubling
to you. And as you hold that question in mind,
notice that a little bit ahead of you, buried in
the sand, is a box. As you come to the box, you
can see your hands reaching into the sand and
digging it out and feel what the box feels like—
with the sand and the water in your hands. Rub
your hands over the box and see what it's made
of and how it feels, as you just focus on having
the box in your hand. Know that it's been
placed there, today, for you to find—created
from within yourself—from a positive place in
yourself that knows what to do. And know that
in a minute, when you open the box, there will
be an image, symbol, or message that will relate
to your question and give you some assistance
or information about the answer. Know and
trust that when the box is opened, that some
object, symbol, words, communication—some
message—is there for you to give you insight
into your question and the answer to it.

So if you're ready, you can open the box now
and see what's there. And if you see something
that isn't completely clear or that you don't
fully understand, you can allow the meaning
to come to you in its own time—later today, in
a dream, or any time at all.

9. Then let go and go into silence. Now is the
   time for letting go. Feel the deep relaxation
   and empty mindedness. Know that you have
   calmed and released distracting thoughts and
   addressed a problem that may have troubled
   you, by visualizing the box. You are now free to
   let go. Be still, God said, *and know that I am there.*
   This is not the time to ask for answers to problems, to visualize desires, or struggle with
   things. Detach and let go of everything. Don't
   worry if you become distracted, just go back
   into the silence by releasing the distraction on
   the exhalation of the breath. If you have impres-
   sions or ideas that seem important, you can
   recall them and record them in your journal
   later. Just be still with the intention of being in
   your spirit. This phase is very important. You
   may receive deep answers in response to your
   prayers, but if you do not, just stay in the silence
   for several minutes. Do not look for answers,
   but if they arrive, accept them. Let go of all of
   your desires. Let go and let God take care of
   things. If you hold on to them, they cannot be
   released and healed.

   Now bring those feelings of relaxation and
   any insights you have gained back with you, as
   you leave all of your thoughts and concerns
   with the ocean to take care of them for you.
   Bring back your special object or message from
   your box. You can bury the box back in the sand
   again for another day—until you need to come
   and find it again. And take a moment to give

thanks for this experience—this opportunity—
and accept that you deserve these feelings of
relaxation and peace.

10. Now bring these feelings of relaxation and peace
back with you as you allow yourself to notice
the way that your hands and feet feel now and
the way that your back feels as it rests in the
chair or on the furniture. And you can begin to
move and stretch your hands and fingers and
your feet and toes—and stretch your arms—taking as much time as you need to bring yourself
back now. And when you are ready, you can
open your eyes and come back—now!

You can try other practices once you have established these firmly. You may want to explore Jain Meditation, an Eastern meditation which focuses on the
chakras; the Jose Silva method, which focuses on spiritual healing and using the power of the mind; or a
moving meditation such as tai chi. Try any one that
interests you. Trust that your interest will bring you the
information you need. Once you have established a
practice, stick with it. Choose something that focuses
your mind and your connection to the divine and stick
with it. In time, you will find that you forget about your
body, that your mind becomes blank and free of concerns. In Tibet, this is known as Rigpa, "The beginning
phase of a rich emptiness."

In my personal experience, this emptiness allowed
specific information I needed to come my mind. During meditation, I became increasingly aware that the

sound of my schoolhouse clock had begun to sound like thunder ticking in my ears. It certainly got my attention. Not only had the sound elevated, but in the rhythm of the ticking I was impressed with specific words and information that I needed to assist with my health.

Some mental health professionals become concerned when their patients begin getting such intuitive messages in their quieted minds. They fear that the patients are "hearing voices." They interpret it as a sign of mental illness. Psychiatrist Judy Orloff in the book *Second Sight* explains the difference between intuitive communication and mental illness. Judy had intuitive communication all of her life and entered the field of psychiatry to help others understand these communication processes. It is important to take care of your mental health so that you can safely use spiritual practices to develop your ability to listen to your own spiritual wisdom. With experience and the practice of meditation, you will be able to discern the intuitive messages that you are receiving.

Encouragement Notes

- You have now a clear idea of how to do a *daily practice*
- You can include prayer and meditation in your practice
- The ability to clear your mind and quiet it relieves stress and the physical damage that comes from stress
- Prayer has become a full experience, transformed from earlier concepts

RESOURCES FOR CHAPTER FOUR

Books

Second Sight. Judith Orloff, M.D., Warner Books: NY, 1996.

MAP: The Co-Creative White Brotherhood Medical Assistance Program. Machaelle Small Wright, Perelandra, Ltd.: Warenton, VA, 1994.

Prayer Is Good Medicine. Larry Dossey, M.D., Harper: San Francisco, 1996.

Full Catastrophe Living. Jon Kabat-Zinn, Ph.D., Delta: NY, 1990.

The Bible

Metaphysical Bible Dictionary. Unity Books, Unity Village, MO, 2000.

Music

Stephen Halpern, *Enhancing Creativity*

Kitaro, *Silk Road Suite*

Ludwig Van Beethoven, *Piano Concertos*

Paul Horn, *In Concert*

Brian E. Paulson, *Arc of Light*

Organizations

The Upper Room Living Prayer Center (United Methodist Church)

24-Hour Prayer Line, 1-800-251-2468

5

Sharing
Spiritual Fitness

The moment you notice that you are just an instrument of God: the moment you become like a hollow flute, the wind will blow through you and there will be music.

—Dhyan Yogi

Riches You Will Gain from This Chapter

- Knowledge of the ways that your relationship to God changes all your relationships positively
- Understanding of the role of love and gratitude in Spiritual Fitness
- Understanding of the ways in which Spiritual Fitness can apply to men, women, and children

THE BEST THING WE can do for ourselves and our world is to clear our perceptual screens of static and let our spirits shine brightly. In this state, we attract the highest and best to ourselves. We also act as a beacon for others. In the last chapter on prayer, we learned how our thoughts and thought projections can heal others. In general, the good thoughts and wishes we have for others truly uplift them because we send them a high positive energy. If they are feeling unworthy or too stressed, however, they may block receipt of this energy. Again, we need to be in the best state possible, not only to send good thoughts, but also to receive them.

It becomes more challenging to remain positive and send positive thoughts to others when they are not in a balanced state. What happens when someone in the checkout line is short with you? What about when your partner does not have time for you? Or when your boss favors someone who you know is wasting the company's time? Is it harder to continue to be positive with them? Of course it is. This is because we slip back to operating from our lower chakras where we deal with power and control issues, or to the first mansion as in St. Theresa's castles. We may experience anger, hostility, a desire to manipulate the situation, and feelings of fear and insecurity. We then tend to project that onto the person or situation that triggered the response. The other people involved are also affected, since our wishes for us and others carry a vibrational energy that affects everything around us.

The challenge is to avoid adding fuel to the fire when someone is behaving negatively. If someone is coming from anger and we give anger in return, we magnify that anger and actually make the situation worse. But we need not repress our anger. What has been triggered in us is very likely tied into an old wound or weakness in self-esteem. The situation can become a gift in disguise to show us where we have been hurt in the past and to help us work through it. For example, a family member who usually calls you every week to see how you are suddenly stops calling. You imagine this as a rejection and you begin to feel hurt and abandoned. Is there a bigger abandonment underneath? Is there a time in the past when you felt these feelings? Perhaps when your parents separated or went back to work after having been home? Maybe a best friend who moved and never wrote to you? When you are triggered, look back to see what may be more deeply rooted in the same issue.

When you are triggered, get curious and see what is going on. Embrace the opportunity to see what negative emotions you have stored. You may need professional guidance to help you through the old hurt. You may also find healing by doing the color breathing and deep breathing exercises from chapter 3, and the hypnotic trance exercise from chapter 2.

Don Miguel Ruiz's *The Four Agreements* reminds us not to take things personally. Others' behaviors have little to do with us and a great deal to do with them. It is often our feelings of insecurity or weak places in our self love that cause us to feel damaged by others. Most often, these events trigger our old patterns that are learned early in life. Our responses are usually about patterns our parents or caretakers learned early in their lives and passed onto us. This can go back many generations and is usually a deeply ingrained pattern that may now be activated in us. It is not too late to change though, as we will see later in this chapter.

For now, be aware that many of your reactions to others are largely based on old patterns and hurts. Be compassionate to the child you once were who experienced the hurt. Practice the breathing exercises to help heal the hurt. Take care of and love yourself in ways that you want to be taken care of now or in ways that you wanted to be taken care of in the past. Take time to see the connections to your original hurt and sadness. Face what happened and how it made you feel, and heal the hurt.

If you feel that professional help will assist you in healing old hurts or patterns, seek a treatment that will heal the mind, body, and spirit. We have mentioned hypnosis, a tool for empowering yourself in a very positive way. You may choose to do self-hypnosis exercises, such as the ones in the hypnosis section, or seek a psychotherapist trained in using hypnosis.

Another powerful technique that allows our minds to heal from old traumas is Eye Movement Desensitization and Reprocessing (EMDR). It is a therapy technique that was developed by Francine Shapiro. EMDR activates parts of the whole self to work together to process and heal old traumas so that they no longer have a hold on us in the present. It does not matter how long ago the event occurred. There is still a part of the mind that clearly and vividly recalls the event that settled into a pattern. The part of the mind that remembers may not be conscious. Many memories are stored in places that are not in our conscious awareness. Sometimes we just know that something emotionally feels good or feels painful. We do not rationalize that it feels a certain way because we had a certain experience when we were young, we just know how it feels. EMDR can bring the trauma into the mind so that it can be healed.

Give yourself the gift of slowing down long enough to feel your feelings. You may recall that a friend slighted you in school or that your first boyfriend or girlfriend broke up with you. These memories are traumatic if we do not deal with them and heal them at the time. They become patterns and part of our belief systems if we do not clear them. We unconsciously store the information that made us feel that something about us was wrong. We may have accepted a negative belief about ourselves by seeing another person's behavior as a personal attack or affront on us. Remember, it is important not to take things personally.

Every situation is a gift that allows you to gain deep insight and healing. Tune into yourself deeply and allow your intuition to speak to you. Take time to meditate to allow your intuition to strengthen. Take time to do mind washings so that you clear and quiet the mental clamor. Allow your intuition to have a voice that can be heard in your quiet mind. Place yourself in the most highly uplifted place you can at every moment of life. This generally means being the highest and best person you can be in any given situation. This allows the inner voice you hear to be the highest connection with Divine God of the Self. As soon as we start taking things personally, we slip back into our ego and out of this high place.

Gerald Jampolsky, in *Love Is Letting Go of Fear,* explains that fear is the opposite of love. When we are reacting personally, we may respond out of fear. Responding from love is the anecdote for behaving in ways that create fear. Ask yourself what you would do in any given situation if you were reacting from love verses fear.

Many people ask, "Is God a being outside the self or is God within us?" The answer to this question is a very controversial one, and the answer to both questions, however, is yes. A divine intelligence is at the source of the universe. We also have this spark of that divine universe in each of us in the form of our souls. It is only when we forget the divine spirit that we are, that we respond painfully to situations.

When we are triggered, we are seeing aspects of our personalities rather than our divine selves. The divine self, fashioned after the universal intelligence we call God, is perfect. Look at what happens when outside events trigger you. If a friend who normally gives you a Christmas gift does not do so, what do you feel? Is there a five-year old inside you who did not have anyone to pay attention to him/her? If the little child was here now, what kind of loving attention would they need? There is an inner child in all of us that still needs the things of which we were deprived. In the case of the five-year-old who needed attention, a trigger at age 35, 45, or 85 may create a number of responses. You may become angry and demand attention. You may feel unloved and hide. The five-year old still needs the attention, but we have developed a pattern of behavior to cope with unmet emotional needs. Maybe we can find a way to heal the old hurt, release the old pattern, and find love in life where it exists. We can turn our attention from what we do not have to what we do have. If you need to do deep work with your inner child, you may want to consult the work of John Bradshaw. A particularly wonderful book is *Coming Home,* which contains meditations to embrace your inner child at various stages of life.

Again, the responsibility comes back to us. This awareness is essential at this point because without it we cannot attain Spiritual Fitness. Conversely we cannot share Spiritual Fitness until we live it. Surely, our mortal selves are not perfect. The path of Spiritual Fitness is a lifetime path. But we can move ourselves into a place where we have gained enough self love and completed enough healing to be able to give the same to others. We will now focus on some of the ways to do just that.

LOVE AND GRATITUDE

> Make ye a joyful noise unto the Lord . . . enter into his gates with thanksgiving and into his courts with praise; be thankful upon him and bless his name.
>
> —Psalm 100: 3, 4

THAT WHICH WE ATTEND to multiplies. One of the simplest examples of this is with children. When we give them attention for some behavior, they continue to exhibit the behavior. This works for and against them. If they exhibit positive behavior and we praise them, they are likely to continue to exhibit the behavior. If we only give them attention when they misbehave, they will continue to misbehave. Negative attention feels better than none at all.

Now let us apply the rule of multiples to Spiritual Fitness. If you have a seed of good in your life, no matter how small, and you feed it and water it, it grows. One of the most powerful ways to feel good is with gratitude. Thank God for all the good in your life, give thanks for good health, friends, income ... whatever is in your life. It is easy to look at what is wrong in your life, but attending to the negative only increases the negative in your life. While you are seeing the downside of something, you are visualizing and affirming it. This does not mean you should ignore your feelings, only to focus on feeding the seeds you most want to grow. Give attention to the positive, give gratitude and thanks.

If you look at your life, you can see how you fuel it. Do you fuel it with positive attention and gratitude, or do you affirm what is wrong with it? Are you putting the high-test fuel into your tank, or lead? My friend Gino, a hairdresser, tells all of his clients that at the beginning of every day, you start out with two empty buckets: a positive bucket and a negative bucket. See which you fill during the day. Notice what you say and how you think and how you behave. At the end of the day, hopefully, your positive bucket is full. While it is human, perhaps, to put some things into the negative bucket, it is the balance of overwhelmingly positive thoughts that should carry you.

If you look at your life, it is a reflection of what you have projected, affirmed, and visualized. You could complain and increase what is wrong or give gratitude and increase what is right. Giving gratitude stirs the kind of positive emotion needed to bring about your good.

The same is true with love. When you give unconditional love in your thought projections, you attract unconditional love back. Do not be concerned with its sources. Not everyone is loving themselves enough to be able to give love back. Just know that it will return and expect it. Expect it in unexpected ways and places. It is a spiritual law that this love will return. Similar vibrations attract one another. If you have always believed that what goes around, comes around, you are right.

FOR WOMEN AND THE PEOPLE WHO LOVE THEM

God is . . . in women and men. The light of the divine has no gender.

—Joan D. Chittister, Marcus Borg, and Ross Mackenzie, *God at 2000*

UNTIL THE PERIOD OF the feminist movement, women were faced with an image of God as a patriarch. The idea of a father/mother God grew as feminist spirituality groups evolved. The idea of the feminine God is one of a nurturing and nourishing one. When we divide God between male and female, we may feel like children of divorced parents. If God is truly our source, our parent, it seems that God would have both genders' traits. In Eastern spiritual teachings, God is beyond gender.

The women of the baby boomer generation have the greatest task of any women at any time in history.

The Neanderthal woman's task of keeping the cave fires burning cannot compare to the job of clearing away the programming of her ancestors from the beginning of time to the present. Today's women are changing the truth of their gender, which is embedded in their minds, hearts, bodies, and genes. They are transforming a reality that once formed the truth of a new generation.

How? By sifting through the messages mothers and grandmothers gave us about ourselves as women, and the messages that the men in our lives gave us about ourselves as women. We take the truths and strengths and let go of all that keeps us from shining our light in the world.

Limiting beliefs about women was one of the biggest blocks I had to overcome on my path. It required releasing many generations' belief systems. Many I kept because they felt true to my feminine nature, but many I did not keep. Once I released the erroneous beliefs, I felt as free as a bird. Keeping the ones that were true to my nature felt good, too. Even as I write, I know the deep satisfaction of spending an evening in my kitchen. At the same time, I continue to sever myself from all beliefs of limitation. Old beliefs may have indicated that a woman could not do certain things because of her gender. If Mother Teresa had accepted all of the limitations of her ancestors, she would never have saved the dying people of India, "one at a time."

Many women today, particularly those of the baby boomer generation, have tried to live out the domestic dreams transferred to them through training and maybe even genetic structure. Sixty percent have failed and have either doggedly tried again or reexamined the dreams and myths from which they must awaken. Trying again is much like banging into a brick wall, backing up and heading toward the wall again. After too many tries, we are scarred and hurt and have too many wounds from which to recover. It is like trying to wear someone else's shoes; they just do not fit.

If our families persist in measuring us by how well we live up to their myths, we may continue to feel diminished in our own eyes. It is only when we begin to sift and sort, keeping what is good and leaving behind the rest that we wake up from the dreams we were given and begin to be fully alive. We begin to be ourselves, our true selves, our highest selves, not the negative programming or limitations we may have been given.

In Madonna Kolbenschlag's book *Kiss Sleeping Beauty Goodbye,* the myths about women are examined. She reviews all the limiting beliefs women got from fairy tales and families and shows how they can liberate themselves from them. Peeling off layers of expectations from our ancestors, associates, and cultures is a task begun by women of the current generation. These are the women who bought the self-help books, used the yoga tapes, and attended the therapy sessions reflecting endlessly on the changes in consciousness that were possible for the very first time in the history of women. The task seemed daunting given the length, strength, and depth of the old programming of the past.

The degree of change we achieve is equal to the commitment we make to our intention and desire for change. It may be the greatest service we can lend to the spiritual journey and to the spiritual upliftment of the world. We can save the beauty of our ancestral culture while becoming free of the bondage from a way of life which no longer serves us or the world.

When we awaken from old dreams about money, appearances, and roles, and decide to give our children a legacy of spiritual love and guidance, we can change the world. If we go out and do volunteer work but do not change our consciousness, we still cannot pass new energy to future generations in a clear field of the mind, body, and spirit. We do not reach a state of health that future generations can model, and we do not blaze new paths on which future generations can walk. We can donate money for food, strength to build habitats, and words of comfort, yet without leaving spiritual food behind, our efforts are limited. It does not mean we should discontinue our positive actions toward humanity, it only means that we start at home. We clean the cobwebs from our own minds and hearts by healing the old programs and allowing our inner light to shine. As more beacons of light fire up their warmth, then a change can occur across the world. The bright light of all the evolved people can act as a magnet for change in others.

If we look at the programming that does not serve us, and the amount of time we spend trying to live up to old expectations, we can imagine what a powerhouse of energy exists inside of us. Let us not direct that energy towards someone else's image of what we should be as women, daughters, wives, mothers, and professionals. Rather, why not heal and redirect ourselves? A goal of reflecting our spiritual infinite energy is a path that can last for a lifetime.

FOR MEN AND THE PEOPLE WHO LOVE THEM

> God is not maleness magnified. God is life without end.
>
> —Joan D. Chittister, Marcus Borg,
> and Ross Mackenzie, *God at 2000*

MEN HAVE BEEN GIVEN their roles and responsibilities for so many generations: make money, support the family, do not show emotion, press on toward your career goals, do not let anyone stand in your way, go it alone, isolate yourself, and be strong. The "boy code," as a friend of mine calls it, is learned early and well and extends into manhood with tentacles that touch men's health, relationships, hearts, and work.

The competitive biological and psychological nature of men tells them they can only succeed by shutting out others, who threaten to take their time, their job, and their friends, if they let them. But how about a world where letting others in is a path to winning for everyone?

Robert Bly authored many books for men that began to change the way men viewed themselves. Expression of feelings became a critical part of maleness, versus the armoring that men did traditionally to avoid feelings. When men get inside the male self and feel the feelings there, they can awaken to feelings of aliveness.

Near Pittsburgh, there is a weeklong retreat modeled after the original retreat developed by Joseph Jastrab that suggests there is another way. The "Hero's Journey" breaks the myths of isolation and separation that men have been given. In the retreat the men tackle physical challenges in a safe, supportive environment where they can be their true selves. The men face and express fear, self-doubt, and a need for support from other men. They ask for these things from their peers and are given it in return. They learn that, with support, they can accomplish what may have been impossible without it. The inner emotions brought to the surface free men to feel their feelings, accept their feelings, and express them without fear of rejection or shame. The shame men were taught to feel for having feelings at all begins to melt away and healing takes place. Men may experience true courage for the first time; the old bravado of ego and false courage falls away to be replaced by a genuineness of self that is far more effective.

This gives us a model for what men may truly be without the limitations of past history. Ever since men went out hunting to bring back food for their families who lived in the caves, men were taught that in order to do that job, they had to be cut off from themselves, cut off from the vast and wonderful resources that exist within the male consciousness. In addition, men were taught that other men may destroy them to protect their survival. No wonder men have been socialized to compete!

Perhaps this "Hero's Journey" can serve as a model for men who want to experience a greater self-realization. The works of Joseph Campbell and Clarissa Pinkola Estés will give a great deal of insight and information into the rich psyches of men and ways in which they can evolve and be truly expressed. Jean Shinoda Bolen, M.D., has written a book for men, *Gods in Everyman,* and one for women, *Goddesses in Everywoman.* These works explain personality archetypes that are prevalent in women and men and the ways in which they express themselves in the world. Recognizing archetypes that we may be playing out is one of the most valuable things that we can do in self-understanding. These books are a wonderful place to begin to change the deep emotional programming or to simply understand it and see how we are living it out.

FOR THOSE WHO LOVE CHILDREN

Let the little children come to me, and do not hinder them, for the Kingdom of God belongs to such
as these.

—Jesus Christ, Luke 18:16

FROM THE START OF my own path to Spiritual Fitness, I
have worked with children's spiritual lives. Children
are in a perfect position to develop a healthy, spiritual
awareness without having to undo years of misconceptions, repressions, or negative experiences. They
can quickly learn relaxation techniques and the ability
to slow the nervous system to heal the self. It has been
my observation that children can reach levels of relaxation and meditation in about six weeks, levels that
adults typically learn in six months. They are in just
the right place to become aware of their natural sense
of spirit. Many children are already in touch with this
sense of their spirit. It is only experience that tends to
suffocate this awareness.

Based on my hypothesis that the children could
benefit from breathing, stretching, and relaxation, I
developed a curriculum of "Mastering Relaxation" for
kids. The curriculum was tested locally, then marketed
internationally. The curriculum consists of a relaxation videotape and audio tapes and adult-directed
lessons. The effect of the techniques was studied while
children were exposed to ten minutes of daily adult-
directed relaxation. This occurred after two introduc-

tory lessons, each forty-five minutes in length. After one month of practice, the children showed a reduction in observable symptoms of stress.

For children, an understanding of the feeling or connection they have to a higher power assists in uplifting them from an ordinary life. The value of a spiritual life creates an inner peace that forms a foundation for all other values. In Annette Hollander's book *How to Help Your Child Have a Spiritual Life*, she discusses the many ways that we can support children in creating their inner peace and spiritual values. Children often have mystical experiences. Many children have reported seeing guardian angels. The high level of joy and peace that children exude tends to be a reflection of their own mystical experiences. They have a sense of being in touch with everything, and this is particularly obvious in their love of nature.

Children can also begin to be in touch with their spirit through prayer and intuitive guidance with their problems. Children often are in touch with their intuition or their inner sense of what is right. They may have to act against their own sense of right and wrong because of the expectations of others in their society. It is important that we allow children to keep this sense of innocence in connection to the spirit. It is what we as adults may spend our entire adult lives trying to recapture. Let us help children to keep that feeling and that knowing.

If children follow a particular religious school or attend a Sunday school experience or join the choir, they can become familiar with organized religion as one way to have a spiritual life. Family unity is also a wonderful way for children to begin to understand their spirituality. Families that pray together, do activities together, and communicate values of love, fairness, kindness, and helpfulness will greatly enhance children's ability to remain connected to their spirit.

Modeling is one of the most important and powerful influences in the world today. Parents are one of the primary role models that children have. As parents we cannot be passively faithful. We have to demonstrate and live our faith and trust in whatever we believe to be the higher self. In this way, children can model our own behavior and not simply be expected to live up to what we say.

School is a supplement that reinforces what is lived at home. You may wish to have your child attend a school that is spiritually, or more creatively based, in order to create this kind of supplementation. When my little nephew prays, he has no doubt that his prayers will be answered. On one occasion, he was praying for me and later called to find that his expectations had been realized. At another time he was very disappointed that my elderly uncle, who was nearing the time for his transition into the afterlife, had not yet been healed. When asked what he did not understand, he said, "Well, why didn't he get well? I prayed for him!"

The innocence and faith of children is a powerful tool for manifestation. They energize their faith and their connection to the higher power through prayer. This is a vast area of energy that must be allowed to continue to exist. Keeping the spirit of children alive is critical.

Children's awareness of religion and spirituality occur differently at different ages. From birth to age two, children are merely learning to use their senses, their eyes, their ears, and to talk, touch, and taste everything. In the two- to six-year range, children are in a "prereligious" state where they are using their imaginations and their beliefs in fairy tales. It is not too early to begin to tell them stories about religious leaders and to read them Bible stories or stories from your own religious system. Once they reach the seven-to-eleven-year range, they are at a level of maturity to develop a religious or spiritual belief system. Imagination has gone the way of reality, and they can separate fantasy from truth. At this point, they are highly receptive to understandings about spiritual and religious pathways. After the age of twelve, they begin to develop their own personal religious thoughts and insights. This is when they become individuated as people, with their own attitudes, beliefs, ideas, and philosophies. For this reason, teenagers may become rebellious, as they establish their own sense of self. While it is necessary to set boundaries for children, it is also important to encourage their growth and movement toward a personal idea of spirituality.

We can also look at children's motivations and their needs at different ages. These are reflected in Lawrence

Kohlberg's *Stages of Moral Development*. They relate to children's motivation in their spiritual behavior. By focusing on Kohlberg's understanding of the moral development of children, we can see how to nurture their spirituality in each age range.

From birth to age seven, children are highly motivated to avoid punishment. It is at this time when we must be careful to give them a great deal of positive attention. We do not want them to learn that punishment is positive attention by ignoring them unless they misbehave. At this stage, we are shaping children's beliefs and feelings about who they are as either "good" or "bad." It is important for children to know that they are good, even if they misbehave. It is important for them to know that they are not flawed or imperfect in their spirit.

Beginning at age eight and moving into age nine, children begin to understand mutual benefit and personal needs. It is at this age that they can do something for someone else because it benefits them and because it benefits the other person. This sense of mutuality is an excellent instinct that we can build upon in the eight- to nine-year age range. Children at this time are able to understand the "golden rule" of treating others as you would want to be treated.

At age ten and beyond, children develop group values. They tend to believe that what is right is defined by the group. If the group plans to go to a certain place at a certain time and that's the "in" place to be, the other children in the group will value that decision. At this time, it is important to be sure that children are involved in positive groups. Spiritual youth groups at churches are good outlets for children who are looking to establish a group sense of value. Directing them toward a spiritual values set is important for a ten-year-old. After age ten, children develop an understanding of what is best for all. The higher or highest good becomes the most important good because it is right for the child and right for the principle itself.

As children move beyond age ten, and into the higher sense of who they are, they can understand that doing what is best for everyone can be best for themselves. They develop a personalization or personification of God. It is at this time that following a religious pathway can be a fulfilling experience for them. Children, however, must be taught to respect all religious pathways and to understand that there is not a Jewish God, a Christian God, an Islamic God, or any other god that allows them to feel separate from others in the world. Children want and need to feel separate and individual in order to feel special and unique. It is fine for them to do so in a personal fashion, and at the same time, to understand that spiritually, we are all the same.

The following relaxation exercises are suitable for children and can be done daily and at any time they are needed.

Exercise: Relaxation for Children

Goal: To begin a relaxation practice for children.

1. Anytime that you want to relax, the first thing you can do is learn how to control your breathing, so that you breathe in a relaxed way. Anytime you feel nervous or afraid, anytime you are afraid of doing something new or going somewhere new or taking a test, you can relax by controlling your breathing.

2. To breathe in a relaxed way, start now by breathing through your nose—making sure that your mouth is closed. Bring the air in through your nose as you inhale, past your throat, past your chest, and all the way down into the area near your stomach called the diaphragm. The diaphragm is right near your waist. As you exhale, first let the air leave the diaphragm and feel the air come back up through the chest, through the throat, and out the nose.

3. Now, let's try it together. Inhale through your nose, bringing the air past your throat and chest into your diaphragm, just like you would fill a balloon with air. Imagine that there's a balloon in your diaphragm and that you can fill it each time that you breathe in or inhale. You might want to put a favorite toy on your diaphragm and feel it rise as you inhale and then come back down as you exhale, inhaling through your nose, bringing the air past your chest, into the diaphragm. Then bring your breath back up

through your chest and throat and out your
nose, just like you were filling a balloon with
air. Inhale through your nose, slowly and
deeply, and bring the breath into your
diaphragm. Now, exhale, and bring your
breath back out of your diaphragm.

4. Now, in order to relax, we will continue to
breathe this way—only more slowly. The best
way to slow down nervousness, tension, and
stress is to slow your breathing. Inhale again
and exhale again, this time to a slow count of
four. Ready? Inhale 2, 3, 4, exhale 2, 3, 4. Relax.
Good. And we'll try it again. Inhale 2, 3, 4, and
exhale 2, 3, 4. Very good! Now, try it again—on
your own—to the count of four. That's right.
Counting in slowly to the count of four and
exhaling, slowly, to the count of four. Remember that whenever you need to slow down and
relax, you can use this way of breathing.

5. Now, continue breathing very slowly, and you
can relax even more by imagining yourself
floating on a cloud. In your mind, picture
and remember what a cloud looks like. You
can remember a time when you may have been
watching a cloud or just imagine a cloud the
way you want it to look. Imagine what color the
cloud is. Today, in your imagination, you can
make the cloud any color you want. Now imagine yourself getting on the cloud, getting comfortable, and sitting or lying down on it. Take a
deep breath as you lie on the cloud—inhaling 2,
3, 4 and exhaling 2, 3, 4. Relax on the cloud, as

it floats in the air and carries you slowly and
gently away from any tension, anxiety, or worry.
See yourself floating on the cloud and notice
the way that you feel. Now just float on the
cloud, breathing deeply, letting go of all your
concerns until you hear my voice again. Very
good! Remember, anytime that you need to, you
can come back and visit your cloud in order to
relax.

6. Now remember where you are and where
you're sitting and notice the feeling of the chair
against your body or the floor if you're lying
down, and bring yourself back slowly to where
you are. In order to help you, I'll count to five.
One, rub your hands together until you have a
feeling of warmth in the palms of your hands.
Two, place your hands over your closed eyes and
feel the warmth from your hands entering into
the back of your eyelids. Three, open your eyes
into the palms of your hands. Four, bring your
hands down. And five, stretch your arms above
your head—feeling relaxed and ready to go on. If
you continue to breathe slowly throughout the
rest of your day, you can maintain this sense of
relaxation until the next time.

Exercise: Visualization

Goal: To visualize a past relaxation in order to become calm in the present.

1. Today, we'll relax on our own and with our family, group of friends, or class in school. You can pick any group that you would like to relax with, that you enjoy being with today. Begin your relaxation with your breathing exercise—to slow you down and begin to let go of stress—inhaling, 2, 3, 4 and exhaling 2, 3, 4. Relax. Each time that you let go of your breath, you can let go of stress or worry. Again, inhale 2, 3, 4, and exhale 2, 3, 4. That's right!

2. As you relax, remember a time when you felt very calm and quiet or think of your favorite place to relax. As you think, remember a time when you felt relaxed and calm. Maybe relaxing at home or on a vacation. Remember that time now. Remember everything about it—remember where it was and how it looked. Remember what you were thinking and feeling as you relaxed. Notice any sounds that you could hear or any smells around you. Now, for a minute, imagine yourself in your favorite place of relaxation. Hear and see that place, and relax until you hear the sound of my voice again. Relax. Relax, and anytime that you want to relax, imagine your favorite place of relaxation and see yourself there.

3. Now, let's imagine during our relaxation today
   that we can relax with a group of others—
   friends, family, classmates—anyone that you
   feel especially comfortable with. And let's relax
   together—to help each other to become calm
   and to feel strong, relaxed, and capable. Focus
   again on feeling relaxed by slowly counting your
   breath to a count of four, inhaling 2, 3, 4, and
   exhaling 2, 3, 4. Good. Now, try it again on
   your own . . . and exhale. Now, imagine that
   your family and friends are with you and that
   you are on a very quiet beach with just you and
   your group of family or friends. See yourself
   walking on the beach with your family and
   friends, walking in the sand, feeling the water
   come up around your feet, and the warmth of
   the sun shining down on you. Now, see everyone in your group walking along the beach
   together. Notice if there is anyone who does not
   seem to be relaxed, and help them to feel relaxed
   now.

4. Let's do some breathing exercises alongside that
   person—to see them becoming relaxed and letting go of tension each time that they exhale.
   Inhale 2, 3, 4, exhale 2, 3, 4. Relax! Now, see
   everyone experiencing the warmth from the
   sun and feeling strong, relaxed, and capable
   together. See everyone in the group able to do
   well—able to get along well—able to do their
   relaxation exercises with the group or on their
   own, when you're together, or when you're not.
   See yourself and everyone else letting go of ten-

sion as they breathe and being able to do that
anytime that they need to. Feeling calm, in control of yourself, relaxed, and capable of bringing
this sense of calm and relaxation with you any-
where and anytime that you need to.

5. Whenever you want to feel this way, just say to
   yourself, "Relax and remember to let go of anything that you don't need." Coming back now
   and bringing these feelings with you, as I count
   to five. One, rub your hands together until you
   have a feeling of warmth in the palms of your
   hands. Two, place your hands over your closed
   eyes and feel the warmth from your hands in
   the back of your eyelids. Open your eyes into
   the palms of your hands at the count of three.
   Four, bring your hands down. And five, stretch
   your arms over your head—feeling relaxed,
   refreshed, and ready to come back. Now!

Encouragement Notes

- Now gratitude and thanks are a part of your prayer practice
- Gratitude multiplies your good many times
- You can relate Spiritual Fitness to men, women, and children
- You can do relaxation exercises with the significant children in your life

RESOURCES FOR CHAPTER FIVE

Books

Return to Love. Marianne Williamson, Harper Collins: NY, 1992.

Love and Survival. Dean Ornish, M.D., Harper Collins: NY, 1998.

Love Is Letting Go of Fear. Gerald Jampolsky, Celestial Arts: Berkeley, CA, 1979.

The Future of Love. Daphne Rose Kingma, Doubleday: NY, 1998.

Goddesses in Everywoman. Jean Shinoda Bolen, M.D., Harper and Row: NY, 1985.

Gods in Everyman. Jean Shinoda Bolen, M.D., Harper Perennial, NY 1989.

If the Buddha Dated. Charlotte Kasl, Ph.D., Penguin: NY, 1999.

How to Help Your Child Have a Spiritual Life. Annette Hollander, M.D., Bantam: NY, 1982.

Smart Learning: Why Learning Is Not All in Your Head. Carla Hannaford, Ph.D., Great Oceans: Arlington,VA, 1995.

Children Under Stress. Louis Chandler, Ph.D., Charles C. Thomas: Springfield, IL, 1982.

Women Who Run with the Wolves. Clarissa Pinkola Estés, Ph.D., Ballantine: NY, 1992.

Music

Jim Bajor, *Somewhere in Time*

Johannes Brahms, *Symphony No. 2*

Maurice Ravel, *Tristan and Isolde*

Twinkle, Twinkle, Little Star

Nancy Mramor, *Relaxation for Children*

6

Beyond Spiritual Fitness

There are two ways to live your
life. One is as though nothing is
a miracle. The other is as though
everything is.

—Albert Einstein

Riches You Will Gain from This Chapter

- Understanding faith and miracles
- Getting to know your angels
  and spiritual guides
- Knowledge of life after death
- A journey through my path toward
  Spiritual Fitness

MIRACLES

TWO THOUGHTS CANNOT OCCUPY the same space at the same time. It is difficult to both believe in miracles and not believe in them. A friend went to a neurologist for an examination. When the doctor asked her to recall details of a story he was about to read, she told him she never remembered what she heard. He responded that she might have difficulty with the test, then, because her preconception about her poor memory would be in the way of her remembering the story. The doctor said she could not mentally entertain the details of the story and, at the same time, a belief in her poor memory.

For the sake of faith, let us "suspend our disbelief." In our state of suspended disbelief, we can put aside our logical, concrete ideas about fantasy and reality, about what is possible and what is not, about practical realities versus spiritual interventions, and we can focus—for a time—on miracles.

It is normal to disbelieve in miracles, unless there is some proof of them. One form of proof of which many people are aware comes in the form of miraculous healing, or what is known as spontaneous remission. A spontaneous remission is a case of rapid healing from a normally fatal illness. It shows how the mind and body are linked and how the faith factor works. Spontaneous remission is defined as "the disappearance . . . of a disease or cancer, without medical treatment or with treatment that is considered inadequate to produce the resulting disappearance of disease symptoms . . ." These remissions occurred: 1) with no treatment (pure remission), 2) with insufficient treatment, or 3) with spiritual cures having been administered. These spiritual cures, such as the ones documented at Lourdes, in France, are sudden, complete, and without medical treatment (*Noetic Sciences Review* #26). The Institute of Noetic Sciences has published the world's largest database of medically reported cases of spontaneous remission in the world.

Some cases of healing involve the use of relaxation and visualization that I covered in an earlier chapter. Visualizing for healing involves becoming quiet and centered and picturing the body well. In a healing session, after entering a state of relaxation, you begin to see the cells well and tell the body to produce healthy cells. A decision to be well accompanies these efforts. Then, you disown the illness: don't call them "*my* allergies" or "*my* brain tumor." Your decision to be well means that you stop telling people you are sick and do not use illness as an excuse to get out of anything or to obtain something. You may miss the attention that sick people receive and the exceptions that are made for them. Pay very close attention to your reactions to this change in attitude. What do you gain by staying sick? When in life did you learn that illness was a strategy that one could use to avoid something, affect someone, or learn something? From whom did you learn it? The mind is a large contributor to creating illness. Illness can be an opportunity to see what your attitudes are. This applies to annoyances such as joint pain, as much as to life-threatening illnesses.

In Louise Hay's book *Heal Your Body,* she connects specific attitudes with specific illnesses. An explanation of our beliefs shows us how our attitudes may be creating a condition in the body that allows illness to develop. As you picture the characteristics of the attitudes and place those attitudes in your body, you may notice what physical conditions can occur. For example, feelings of being defeated in our efforts often weaken the immune system. An attitude of rigidity can lend itself to arthritis. An overly generous or stingy heart can relate directly to problems in that organ. As we release our self-destructive attitudes our body lets go of the behaviors and biological reactions related to the attitude.

Relinquishing the gain and special consideration given to sick people makes it no longer convenient or desirable to be ill. These are all ways in which the mind heals the body without medical intervention. *Getting Well Again,* by Carl Simonton and Stephanie

Matthews Simonton, explains how to use imagery for healing. The life of Norman Cousins, author of many books, has been chronicled to show how attitude, and especially laughter, can heal even terminal illnesses.

THE SPIRIT OF FAITH AND PRAYER

Prayer . . . is the facing of life's exigencies . . . is not cowering before these circumstances, but rather meeting them with courage.

—Bishop John Shelby Spong,
Why Christianity Must Change or Die

WHEN WE PRAY IN affirmative ways, we acknowledge and activate the universal spirit that is in everyone. We connect with everyone and with the divine. We see how our spirit gives us life and surpasses any individual personal cause for illness. Joan Borysenko tells us about Ivan Pavlov, a famous psychologist. He was told that he was about to die. He asked that he be brought a bucket of mud. As he was making mud pies he remembered making them as a child at the river where his mother washed clothes. He felt a joy that produced a "healing feeling of connection" with all of life and a spontaneous remission occurred.

It is the giving over of all our personal worry to belief in the spirit which allows our bodies to move and to heal. It is the awareness that we are vehicles for God to pass through. And as such, if we stop controlling our lives long enough to get out of our own way, the passage can occur. This is why childlike innocence, laughter, and prayer allow healing to occur in the body and the emotions. Faith is knowing that God is there and does move through you. Faith is the form of continual prayer in which your belief constantly affirms God's presence in your life.

This faith goes beyond the miraculous healing of the body. What about healing of the mind and emotions? Can you recall having an understanding, awareness, or insight that was so important that it changed your life? These changes can heal our hearts, our relationships with others, our careers, our finances, or just our feelings about life. If you have not had these insights, begin a path to Spiritual Fitness. You will have them!

Faith reflected in the body can have a direct and open connection that works through the mind. One of the best examples of these phenomena is the "placebo effect." A placebo is a substance that has no healing power, but which a person believes, in fact, does have that power. In placebo studies, approximately one third of the individuals taking the placebo tend to get well without other interventions. Placebo works in reverse also. When patients in one study believed they were receiving chemotherapy, they experienced hair loss and nausea.

And what about the role of the doctor? Does the healer's attitude matter? Yes. In a study of doctor's

attitudes, some patients were routinely given a medication by doctors who offered no comments, positive or
negative, about the medication's effectiveness. Other
patients had "enthusiastic doctors" who told them
how effective the medication was and how excited they
were about the medicine's results. The results showed
that patients of enthusiastic doctors benefited more
from the treatment. If is often our belief in a treatment
that makes it most effective.

Sometimes, as spiritually evolved as we may become
and as deeply as we transform our attitudes, we can
still experience illness or loss. Illness is not necessarily
self-created or unconsciously attracted. Jesus died on
the cross, Buddha died of food poisoning, and Krish-
namurti died of pancreatic cancer. This awareness can
help us to avoid blaming ourselves too much when we
become sick.

ANGELS AND SPIRITUAL GUIDES

Angels are regularly mentioned in the Koran . . . in
Judaism and in Christianity . . . as messengers of
God.

—James R. Lewis and Evelyn Dorothy Oliver,
Angels A to Z

WE HAVE REVIEWED THE different spiritual beliefs and
psychological techniques which support a healthy
mind and body and allow the spirit to be at the hub of

our wheel of life. While I have reported some very mystical experiences in prior chapters, there has also been logical support for these experiences. What about experiences that defy logical explanation? What about a faith-based belief in the intangible, unexplainable miraculous events that are possible in our lives? Some of the realities of our experiences are based in faith—even in religious experience. For example, during Hanukkah, Jews celebrate the fact that oil, which was expected to last one day, lasted for nine days. In Christianity, it is believed that Jesus was born, immaculately conceived in the womb of the Virgin Mother Mary. Even in our accepted religious systems, miracles are widely accepted proof of the existence of God's blessing in our lives.

What about today, right now? Can we uplift ourselves enough to experience this level of blessings? I believe we can. Even Jesus said, "These things that I do, you can do, and even greater." We will not do it through the ego or pride. The ego mostly gets in the way and blocks these experiences. But we can obtain these blessings through a humble surrender of our lives to the Spirit of God and ourselves. Now all things are possible!

We have assistants in our lives, usually unseen, who guide us when we are willing to listen. This does not mean they guide us away from all troubles and trials. These trials are often the growth experiences which bring us to a higher good and strip away our old misconceptions. These messengers and guides help us navigate through the tough times and allow us to move through life's maze with some direction.

In biblical literature, angels are prominent messengers from God that bring truths from God and miracles of protection. My grandmother Amelia, who always had the faith and innocence of a child, loved to tell the story of the time she was holding her newborn daughter, standing at the top of her spiral staircase. She tripped and fell to the bottom. As she fell, holding tight to her baby, she felt as though she was held in the arms of angels. It was like "floating on a cloud" she said. She arrived at the bottom without a scratch or bruise on either herself or the child. At another time, she "smelled the roses" of Saint Teresa as she was praying for her son during the Second World War. (It is believed that when Saint Teresa brings a miracle into your life, the air around you is filled with a strong scent of roses.) Soon, her son came home from the war and was uninjured and safe. Faith makes miracles. I can recall a time when I was driving and had dropped a pen onto the floor of my car. As I glanced down to find it, I felt a hand atop my right hand. It felt as though it picked up my hand and placed in on the gearshift. My hand then moved the gear shift into the park position. I looked up to see that the car had drifted to a stop right in front of a three-foot high cement medial strip. In another second, I would have crashed into it. The hand of God is everywhere, especially when we open ourselves to it.

Sophy Burnam has written wonderful books about angels. In David Goddard's book *The Sacred Magic of the Angels,* specific signs of angel's presence are given. We are told how to pray to the angels Gabriel, Raphael, Michael, and the others, accomplishing tasks such as blessing a home, shielding and protecting yourself, and increasing prosperity. Goddard also offers signs of the angel's responses to us. Having a picture or reproduction of an angel in your meditation area can act as an invitation to receive angel blessings during meditation.

Spirit guides are thought of as beings who may have once physically lived on the earth and who now act as guides or protectors. In Catholicism, each person has a "patron saint" who is their namesake, who is believed to be their personal guide. In Native American spirituality, ancestors who have passed away are believed to act on behalf of the living. These ancestors are called upon for guidance and assistance. Native American spirits have a kinship to many who are not of Native American descent, as well.

Native Americans name their children after aspects of nature—with names like Gray Wolf, Yellow River, and Running Bear. You may find that a particular symbol continues to show up in your life or that you are attracted to a special symbol from nature. Perhaps you are drawn to yellow roses, to red cardinals, or to sunflowers. Pay attention to these attractions. Spirit guides may try to get our attention in many ways. Perhaps there is a Native American guide working with you.

From birth, I was given a "patron saint" Saint Anna, Jesus' grandmother. I had a great grandmother named Anna and was especially intrigued by my saint. I found out that Anna knew the spiritual value of music, how God works through nature, and the ways of the prophets, and dreamed of being a healer. The inspiration of her life proved to be a wonderful guide for me.

Don't hesitate to call on the angels, saints, spirit guides, or ancestors to guide you in living a spiritual life. Talk to Buddha, Jesus, Abraham, Moses, Sitting Bull, Geronimo, or anyone to whom you feel particularly connected. Often when I am doing psychotherapy with a client, the clients bring their awareness of their own spirit guides to the session with them. They invite their guides to be present and invite the spirit to assist with their healing through the session. More and greater work is done when we stop trying to do it all ourselves and allow our angels to assist us.

LIFE AFTER DEATH

And many of them that sleep in the dust of the earth shall awake . . . to everlasting life.

—Daniel 12:2

IS THERE LIFE AFTER death? I suppose I have always suspended my disbelief about this subject. But when my grandfather's spirit came to see me the day of his funeral, I became a fast believer. What do we know about life after death? Since we are not usually equipped to shift back and forth between life and the afterlife, much of what we know comes from the literature on Near-Death Experiences (NDEs). Many people have had accidents, heart attacks, or other illnesses, and have "died" momentarily—only to come back and report their experiences. Often, they encounter a white light, or report having seen a spiritual being, and are given knowledge and insights that surpass anything they could have ever imagined. My friend's sister Judy had such an experience and reported that she could not recall the content of the conversation that took place with heavenly beings during the near-death experience. She only knew that it had been the most intelligent conversation she'd ever had.

Other research has been done by Dr. Gary Schwartz, a professor at the University of Arizona. Formerly at Yale and Harvard, Dr. Schwartz had a strong interest in life after death and conducted a three year research project. He studied famous mediums who communicated with loved ones who had passed on. Subjects verified that the information brought forth by the mediums from their deceased relatives was indeed accurate. Following the documentation, Dr. Schwartz concluded that without a doubt, there was life after death.

Is there life beyond this world? Often, we have dreams about deceased loved ones. We wonder if, in fact, these are connections or communications from the afterlife. Often, the people in our dreams tell us information that seems very important and meaningful and that strengthens our belief in the afterlife. Much has been written about the afterlife. Dr. Raymond Moody is the pioneer of near-death experience literature. He interviewed as many people as he could find who had had near-death experiences and wrote about them in his textbooks. The experiences he reports are very similar in many ways, and suggest that there is, in fact, an experience that occurs beyond life. Another author, Betty Eadie, shares details of her own near death experience in her book *Embraced By the Light*. Scientists attempt to explain near-death experiences as a chemical or biochemical reaction in the brain, which produces an altered state of consciousness. Clearly, we do not know exactly what happens. Perhaps, in a moment of suspended disbelief, you will experience a dream or intuition that may help you to know about the existence of life after death.

MY TEST ON THE PATH TOWARD SPIRITUAL FITNESS: PART ONE

The two medicines do not have to be antagonists, but for the moment they clearly face in opposite directions.

—Deepak Chopra, *Quantum Healing*

AS I SAT DOWN to write about my test, I attempted to read inspirational books to prepare myself. However, I was unable to concentrate and found myself feeling extremely emotional. I realized that these feelings had been with me since I awoke; I knew that it was the day to tell the story of a personal test on my path of Spiritual Fitness.

By the year 1999, I had been on a spiritual path for over twenty years. I had traveled the world to study different religions, miracles, the mind/body/spirit connection, and all of the elements of Spiritual Fitness that we have talked about in this book. I had been teaching groups and seeing clients using this knowledge and was witness to profound changes.

I was running a meditation group at a local hospital. On the last night of the group, I offered a guided meditation with the intention of leading participants to meet their spirit guides or angels. I calmed and quieted myself to lead the exercise. (Long ago, I learned that the best meditation leaders are in a state of relaxation themselves.) As I led the participants to visualize walking down the beach to meet and converse with their guide, I suddenly experienced a visualization in my own consciousness: while I was picturing the beach, Jesus appeared on the sand. I had not asked for any particular spirit guides to come to me, only to the participants of the group, and I surely did not expect Jesus. I felt a sense that he was telling me that I had the compassion of Christ and a desire to take away others' pain, even if it meant suffering for them myself. Despite the quiet, unconditionally loving and nonjudgmental nature of the message, I still felt it was a subtle warning. Perhaps the characteristic of compassion was somehow out of balance for me. I had not been in touch with the feeling of taking others' pain into myself before that night, but I fully recognized it when it was presented to me.

At the time I did not do anything about it and was working in excess of sixty hours a week. Soon I woke up with swollen lymph nodes the size of quarters in my neck. I consulted two doctors who dismissed them, didn't know what they were, and didn't know what to say about them. The third doctor, an old and trusted friend, recommended a biopsy on one of the lumps if they did not go away. The fourth doctor I consulted ran blood work, and I was diagnosed with mononucleosis. Throughout the next month, I became more and more tired, and by the end of the month I was completely exhausted. I asked more doctors why I was not getting better and they assured me that mononucleosis takes time to heal. By the next night, I felt the swollen nodes all through my body and internal organs. I had so much pain in the area of my liver that I could not sleep. I was black and blue all over and was having spontaneous nosebleeds. No one seemed to know what to do with me. My intuition told me that this was not mononucleosis anymore, no matter what anyone said. I woke up in the morning and went to the emergency room of a local hospital with a suitcase. I was staying until someone found out what was wrong with me.

My decision to go to the hospital was the beginning of a series of incidents in which I would have the balance of my life in my own hands and would have to make life and death decisions. I was admitted to the hospital shortly after they began running tests on me. After a week of biopsies, the medical professionals diagnosed me with a curable form of leukemia, one of the only two diseases known to be curable. The homeopaths, naturopaths, and healers that I knew said this was a gross misdiagnosis. My two worlds had begun to collide. My faith-based practitioners (Eastern Medicine) and medical practitioners (Western Medicine) were not in agreement, and my life was on the line. Only I could make the decisions that needed to be made at this time. My spirit kicked in and took over, but I agonized at each juncture of treatment about what was the "right thing to do." It was time to apply every principle I had ever uncovered on the spiritual path to fitness and begin the road to wellness. The day I was diagnosed with leukemia, I received another vision of Jesus during a Reiki treatment. As I lay with my eyes closed, I could see him pop into my mind. This time, my problem of carrying the compassion of Christ was implied. This time he merely said, "You don't have to die for them, I've already done that for you." I realized that not only had I wanted to absorb their pain but I had identified, somehow, with my illness as a potential cure for what ailed others.

MY TEST ON THE PATH TOWARD
SPIRITUAL FITNESS: PART TWO

Our own inner intelligence is far superior to any
we can substitute from the outside.

—Deepak Chopra, *Quantum Healing*

BECAUSE I WAS IN such critical condition, I agreed to
begin a chemotherapy regimen and was transferred to
a larger urban hospital. My first night at this hospital
was one of the worst nights of my life. By the first
night, I had been set up on intravenous wires and
poles and several chemotherapies were being injected
into my system. By midnight, I felt like my body was
having a major heart attack and a stroke. I thought I
was going to die. The confused-looking intern who
was assigned to me ordered a lot of monitors and tests
and then left the room. He appeared to have no experience with my plight. The nurses, who had a lot of
experience, wore wise looks on their faces but had to
defer to his orders and left the room. Now I not only
felt like I was having a heart attack, I was immobilized
in my room with IVs and monitors all over my body,
afraid of dying from heart failure, and completely
alone.

The next day I asked that my care be assigned to a
more experienced doctor and learned that the horri-
ble symptoms of the night before were reactions to
chemotherapy. No one had warned me about it. If
anyone had, I do not know if I would have agreed to

take the treatment. Professionals also failed to tell me that the treatments would immediately catapult me into menopause with the force of hitting a brick wall.

Each day I watched over my medical treatments, my unemployment and disability benefits, and my healing. Not a day went by that I didn't have to correct or educate my caregivers: "No. I don't usually receive that medicine" or "I'll be needing more of this medicine" or "No, I take this medicine with food" or "I have my food now so I need that medicine." Between the phone in my room and the fax machine at the nurse's station, I negotiated the elaborate bureaucracy to obtain my disability income. It was like running a small business, while fighting for my life. My nurses were more than trained professionals. They were kind, compassionate, wonderful people who felt like a lifeline. They believed me when I told them that although the doctors' orders had indicated I should take certain medicines that he had later rescinded the order and failed to inform them. They knew that I was aware of my body and if I asked to increase or decrease a medicine, that they should ask the doctor if he would give the order to do so. They knew how long, painful, ugly, and lonely the nights were in the hospital. They knew that sometimes a patient asks for something just so that a human being will come and bring it, breaking up the solitude.

Each and every day of the following weeks was filled with pain and hope, drug toxicity and side effects, prayers and healing, friends and family, and loving support. My spirit kicked into high gear. My instincts and intuitions got stronger and my spirit had risen to the occasion.

I sought and received complementary or alternative medicine treatments, even though the hospital officially did not agree with me. Teas were brought to me for nausea, energy workers came to my room to give therapeutic touch and other treatments, and prayer circles and healing ceremonies were held around the city. Healers from around the country conducted distance healing, otherwise known as prayer, and masses were attended by friends everywhere. My spirit enlarged and strengthened and took over my healing. Prayer, faith, and visualization were my tools.

This, I believe, is where the test was on my spiritual path. I had spent the prior twenty-nine years committed to a curriculum of spiritual study and practice. It was time to see if I could use them to save my own life. Faith was my first tool; then, visualization, affirmation, prayer, and support from others. I also had an overlay of medical treatments, which I had previously disdained. Bridging the gap between Eastern and Western medicine was key. I used many vitamins and herbs in a personally and carefully researched manner and chose just the right nutritional plan. It took 150 percent commitment.

I do not know if a force greater than myself decided it was exam time, or if my own spirit saw a need and created the experience. I do know that I decided that it was not going to be final exam time. I heard nurses discussing how rapidly I was recovering. A few days before I was discharged, one of my doctors said I could go home as soon as I had more neutrophils in my blood. This would be a long and difficult task, she explained, since the chemotherapy was killing my blood including my neutrophils. I asked her to draw me a picture of a neutrophil, complete with colored pencils. I phoned my friends and we began visualizing and telling my body how many neutrophils it needed. In a few days, I was released. I went from near death to a full remission in twenty-two days.

Unfortunately my test did not end there. I had to undergo a program of intense chemotherapy and radiation to maintain the remission and catch any undetected disease. After much research I decided to use a combination of traditional and holistic treatments. After several months, the treatments had taken a dramatic toll on my body. I could not even sit up. I was unable to hold down any food or water. I had a twenty-four-hours-a day migraine headache, and my veins were so weakened that when an IV was placed in them, the veins broke. A weird chemical toxicity from the medicine made me feel as though an alien had taken up residence inside my body. My continual task was to live from deep within myself and not identify with the toxic feelings; to hold to my spiritual self and not allow the toxicity of my body to cause discouragement or self pity; and to be my fullest, most faithful and positive self

in the face of my biggest life challenge. I had to entertain only thoughts of wellness in the face of all of the
symptoms of illness and of firm health in every way. I
called upon spiritual energy when I had no physical
energy. I had to know that I was destined to recover.

Throughout this process my intuition strengthened.
After months on maintenance, one of my doctors recommended a life threatening medical procedure
which would have incapacitated me for one to one
and a half years. I was told it would ensure my healing. He stated that my test results had shown that the
procedure was necessary. I intuitively knew this was
askew and asked to see the test results. After waiting
two weeks to get the test report, I sat in my doctor's
office waiting room and would not leave until I saw
the results. They could not produce them, discovering
that not only was there no test results report, but the
test to determine if I needed the procedure had never
even been given. *They were going to perform a life-threatening procedure, without any medical evidence that it was
required, based on nonexistent test results.* I did not care if
it was the fault of the lab, the medical records depart-
ment, or the doctor, but I knew that this was a signal
for me to move on. I consulted with other medical
treatment programs and chose a more holistically oriented physician to finish my treatment.

From the day I checked myself into the hospital,
my spirit took over. I was too sick, too tired, and too
toxic from drug side effects to rely on my mind to

make decisions. My spirit stepped right up and took over, stronger than ever.

Then, I had to know when I was well, when further treatments would have killed me, and when it was time to say no more. I would not take a treatment past the limits of my tolerance, risking death from the treatment itself. Maintenance oral medication was used at my request, with the benevolent participation of a wonderful self-chosen physician. I had found a new doctor who believed that the doctor and patient were partners in the treatment program. And so we were. He used hypnosis for pain management and accepted my treatment preferences when they could be medically supported.

Then came the emotional healing. In psychology, there are personality factors called defense mechanisms. These mechanisms are defenses we hold up around ourselves to preserve our identities. These mechanisms include denial, which is a way of telling ourselves that something is not true when the truth of it would be too powerful to face. This is how we often feel when someone we love has died. Another defense mechanism is sublimation. This mechanism might be used to assign a higher level of motivation to a behavior than the one we have. An example of sublimation would be visiting a sick friend, telling ourselves it is for their benefit, when it is really because we are bored and need company. Defense mechanisms are part of a normal personality. They serve the purpose of allowing us to see only as much as we can handle about ourselves at any given time.

When we dream, our defense mechanisms of our conscious and subconscious mind are loosened and buried material can surface. This is why dreams can be so confusing; they are bits and pieces of information we suppress until we are ready to deal with them. This is why the truth of what is really going on in our lives is suppressed by the mind, only to surface in dreams. We can learn a great deal of truth when we examine our dreams (see chapter 2).

When faced with my own serious illness, I did not have the strength to hold up my defense mechanisms. Material from my subconscious and unconscious flooded into consciousness. I had visions, dreams, and awareness I might never have had otherwise. I saw what my deeply held beliefs and patterns about wellness, life, and people truly were. I had spiritual insights that were mind-boggling, recognizing the truth of these insights each time they appeared. They seemed so obvious once recognized, but had been so deeply buried. I became aware of the burden of my unconscious beliefs that originated with the beliefs of my ancestors. My spirit released much of the burden.

I still do not know now whether the healers and homeopaths were correct in saying that my illness was a misfiring of messages from my DNA to my body, one that could be easily corrected. Maybe the traditional medical doctors were right in their diagnosis of leukemia. Maybe both were looking at the same phenomena from different perspectives, much like we can view God from different sides. What I do know is that I had a roller coaster ride of a spiritual journey, one that uplifted me to a higher faith in Spiritual Fitness. I know that I moved through the test on my path with great spiritual enthusiasm. In Greek, *enthusiasm* means to put God in front. And that is Spiritual Fitness. *Amen!*

Encouragement Notes

- You have completed Spiritual Fitness! May the rest of your journey be all that it could be!

RESOURCES FOR CHAPTER SIX

Books

The Four Agreements. Don Miguel Ruiz, Amber-Allen: San Rafael, CA, 1997.

How to Know God. Deepak Chopra, Three Rivers Press: NY, 2000.

Quantum Healing. Deepak Chopra, Bantam: NY, 1989.

Spiritual Passages: Embracing Life's Spiritual Journey. Drew Leder, M.D., Ph.D., Jeremy Tarcher: NY, 1997.

The Soul's Code: In Search of Character and Calling. James Hillman, Random House: NY, 1996.

The Possible Human. Jean Houston, Jeremy Tarcher: NY, 1982.

The Messengers: A True Story of Angelic Presence and the Return to the Age of Miracles. Julia Ingram and G. W. Hardin, Pocket Star: NY, 1997.

Anna, a Woman of Miracles: The Story of the Grandmother of Jesus. Carol Haenni and Vivian Van Vick, ARE Press: Virginia Beach, VA, 2001.

Love, Medicine, and Miracles. Bernie S. Siegel, M.D., Harper Perennial: NY, 1990.

A Book of Angels. Sophy Burnam, Ballantine: NY, 1990.

Illusions. Richard Bach, Dell: NY, 1977.

Embraced By the Light. Betty J. Eadie, Gold Leaf Press: Placerville, CA, 1992.

Music

Claude Debussy, *Clair de lune*

Evanson, *High Joy*

Georgia Kelly, *Sound of Spirit*

Wolfgang Amadeus Mozart, *Coronation Mass*

ABOUT INNER SPACES
NETWORK, INC.

INNER SPACES NETWORK, INC. is a nonprofit organization that is dedicated to creating programs for at-risk children addressing such issues as stress management, conflict resolution, drug and alcohol prevention, bullying prevention, depression, anxiety, and disability awareness. We are currently seeking contributions to continue our work. If you are interested in providing such assistance or know of someone who may be in need, please contact us at:

Inner Spaces Network, Inc.
100 West Station Square Dr., Suite 230
Pittsburgh, PA 15219
Drmramor@aol.com

Free Magazine

Read unique articles by Llewellyn authors, recommendations by experts, and information on new releases. To receive a **free** copy of Llewellyn's consumer magazine, *New Worlds of Mind & Spirit,* simply call 1-877-NEW-WRLD or visit our website at www.llewellyn.com and click on *New Worlds.*

LLEWELLYN ORDERING INFORMATION

Order Online:
Visit our website at www.llewellyn.com, select your books, and order them on our secure server.

Order by Phone:
- Call toll-free within the U.S. at 1-877-NEW-WRLD (1-877-639-9753). Call toll-free within Canada at 1-866-NEW-WRLD (1-866-639-9753)
- We accept VISA, MasterCard, and American Express

Order by Mail:
Send the full price of your order (MN residents add 7% sales tax) in U.S. funds, plus postage & handling to:
Llewellyn Worldwide
P.O. Box 64383, Dept. 0-7387-0640-X
St. Paul, MN 55164-0383, U.S.A.

Postage & Handling:

Standard (U.S., Mexico, & Canada). If your order is:
$49.99 and under, add $3.00
$50.00 and over, FREE STANDARD SHIPPING

AK, HI, PR: $15.00 for one book plus $1.00 for each additional book.

International Orders (airmail only):
$16.00 for one book plus $3.00 for each additional book

Orders are processed within 2 business days.
Please allow for normal shipping time. Postage and handling rates subject to change.

Authentic Spirituality

The Direct Path to Consciousness

RICHARD N. POTTER

Our world is plagued with problems related to religions that are based on cultural and historical factors. Many people hunger for a practical and reasonable approach to spirituality that does not insult their intelligence. In other words, they are ready for an authentic spirituality of consciousness.

Lifelong mystic Richard Potter explores consciousness-based spiritual paths and demonstrates how the experience of direct mysticism can help you to open your heart and live a life of clarity, joy, peace, and love. Experiment with practices such as meditation, breathwork, sounding, and retreats.

0-7387-0442-3
312 pp., 6 x 9   **$15.95**

The Big Game

10 Strategies for Winning at Life

SCOTT MACMILLAN

Do you enjoy your life? Do you live by your own personal choices? Are you living the life you dreamed of as a child?

If not, you are not alone. Many of us were never taught how to build the strong, personal foundation necessary for living life on our own terms.

The good news is that it's never too late to learn. *The Big Game* will teach you the ten components that anyone can develop to prepare for the "big game" of life, and come out a winner. It's a fresh, innovative strategy based on the author's twenty years of experience teaching health principles, athletics, and the martial arts.

0-7387-0346-X
216 pp., 6 x 9   **$14.95**

Available in Spanish: *El reto de la vida*
0-7387-0401-6
216 pp., 6 x 9   **$15.95**

Energy Sourcebook

The Fundamentals of Personal Energy

DR. JILL HENRY, ED.D.

The unseen world of energy is all around us. Becoming aware of your personal energy is the first step toward understanding and channeling its power. The *Energy SourceBook* can help you discover how energy flow is a source of physical health, prosperity, and happiness.

Experienced in both traditional and alternative medicine, Dr. Jill Henry describes how energy manipulation is a terrific tool for self-healing and transformation. She discusses several energy theories in depth, spanning meditation, feng shui, polarity energy balance, and chakra work. The *Energy SourceBook* also teaches the techniques behind the theories, offering more than 150 simple exercises and activities.

0-7387-0529-2
216 pp., 7½ x 9⅛   **$16.95**

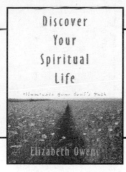

Discover Your Spiritual Life
Illuminate Your Soul's Path

ELIZABETH OWENS

Some are led to the spiritual path by a mystical experience, by a tragic life circumstance, or by nagging feelings of discontent. Whatever the reason, you need a road map or guide to assist you along the way. Spiritualist medium Elizabeth Owens gives you the tools to connect with that higher guidance that, she says, already resides within yourself.

Learn a life-changing method for handling problems and disappointments. Discover effective ways to meditate, pray, create affirmations, forgive those who have hurt you, and practice gratitude. Process painful emotions and thoughts quickly through the art of becoming a balanced observer.

0-7387-0423-7
264 pp., 5³⁄₁₆ x 8   **$12.95**

Choosing Joy, Creating Abundance

ELLEN PETERSON

Millions of people give up on their dreams every day. They believe success is impossible without a stroke of luck, such as winning the lottery. *Choosing Joy, Creating Abundance* offers a ray of sunshine to those who have lost all hope in personal prosperity.

Offering a psychological and spiritual perspective on prosperous living, psychotherapist Ellen Peterson explores the practical dimensions of abundance. She helps readers define their ideas of personal success and overcome the hidden obstacles that often hinder prosperity. Her empowering words, sensible advice, and personal stories illustrate that inner peace and contentment are within everyone's grasp.

0-7387-0543-8
216 pp., 6 x 9 $12.95

Transformative Meditation

Personal & Group Practice to Access Realms of Consciousness

GAYLE CLAYTON

Never underestimate the power of a small group of conscious, committed individuals to change the world. As humanity grows ever more complex, we need to balance technological advances with an evolution of higher consciousness. One way to do that is through group or collective meditation.

This system of meditation creates a single identity that transforms the individuals, the group, and later, the world. Select groups and teachers have already incorporated collective meditation into successful practice. Now, *Transformative Meditation* introduces this system to everyone. It presents an overview of meditation systems, explores the various levels of transformative meditation, and teaches you how to move the group to upper astral planes, how to chant to create a higher identity, and how to increase moments of mystical awareness.

0-7387-0502-0
216 pp., 6 x 9 $12.95

To order, call 1-877-NEW-WRLD
Prices subject to change without notice

Chakras for Beginners

*A Guide to Balancing
Your Chakra Energies*

DAVID POND

The chakras are spinning vortexes of energy located just in front of your spine and positioned from the tailbone to the crown of the head. They are a map of your inner world—your relationship to yourself and how you experience energy. They are also the batteries for the various levels of your life energy. The freedom with which energy can flow back and forth between you and the universe correlates directly to your total health and well-being.

The chakras stand out as the most useful model for you to identify how your energy is expressing itself. With *Chakras for Beginners* you will discover what is causing any imbalances, how to bring your energies back into alignment, and how to achieve higher levels of consciousness.

1-56718-537-1
216 pp., 5⁵⁄₁₆ x 8   **$9.95**

Available in Spanish: *Chakras para principiantes*
1-56718-536-3
216 pp., 5⁵⁄₁₆ x 8   **$9.95**

To order, call 1-877-NEW-WRLD
Prices subject to change without notice

Meditation for Beginners

Techniques for Awareness,
Mindfulness & Relaxation

STEPHANIE CLEMENT, PH.D.

Perhaps the greatest boundary we set for ourselves is the one between the conscious and less conscious parts of our own minds. We all need a way to gain deeper understanding of what goes on inside our minds when we are awake, asleep, or just not paying attention. Meditation is one way to pay attention long enough to find out.

Meditation for Beginners explores many different ways to meditate—including kundalini yoga, walking meditation, dream meditation, tarot meditations, and healing meditation—and offers a step-by-step approach to meditation, with exercises that improve concentration, relax your body quickly and easily, work with your natural healing ability, and enhance performance in sports and other activities. Just a few minutes each day is all that's needed.

0-7387-0203-X
264 pp., 5%6 x 8, illus.   **$12.95**

Available in Spanish: *Meditación para principiantes*
0-7387-0266-8
264 pp., 5%6 x 8, illus.   **$14.95**

To order, call 1-877-NEW-WRLD
Prices subject to change without notice